DESIGNING FOR CHRISTMAS

Carroll Swarm is a Garden Club of America Artistic Flower Show Judge Emeritus, a designer and lecturer experienced in teaching novices, and has been a partner since 1975 in a business specializing in custom-designed dried and silk flower decorations for offices and homes. A major in art, design and sculpture at college, she is a member of the Green Spring Garden Club, The Garden Club of America and the Federated Garden Clubs of Maryland.

DESIGNING FOR CHRISTMAS

A Handbook of Instruction, Information and Illustrations

CARROLL H. SWARM

Photography by Ken Hostetter

Illustrations by Carol Geist

Prospect Hill Press

Baltimore, Maryland

Book designed by Carol Geist
Cover effect created by Artography, Baltimore
Typeset by Brown Composition, Baltimore
Printed in Hong Kong. Thanks, Scott Piazza!

ISBN 0-941526-08-9

Published by Prospect Hill Press
216 Wendover Road
Baltimore, MD 21218
(301) 889-0320

Swarm, Carroll H., 1934-
    Designing for Christmas: a handbook of instruction, information, and illustrations/by Carroll H. Swarm: illustrations by Carol Geist: photographs by Ken Hostetter.
    p. cm.
Includes index.
ISBN 0-941526-08-9: $14.95
1. Christmas decorations.   2. Handicraft.   I. Title.
TT900.C4S93. 1991
745.594′12—dc20   91-22726
                                                        CIP

TABLE OF CONTENTS

Dedicated to the Green Spring Valley Garden Club with fondness and appeciation for many years of learning and friendship.

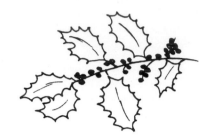

ACKNOWLEDGMENTS

I would like to thank my special neighbors Chris and Bill Pistell and Pat and Jim Fusting for allowing me to descend upon them at Christmas time. A big thank you also to my pinecone providers, Kitty Wagner, Paul Hudson, and Shirley and Larry Silbernagel, who gathered essential cones for me in all manner of weather, wherever they happened to be. I am grateful to Rennie Harrison and Cinny May, my garden club friends, who shared their beautiful boxwood with me, and to Pat Rock who provided me with some much-needed props. I thank those ladies who so graciously allowed me to use their needlepoint works-of-art at this special time of the year: Barbara Budlow, Amy Newhall, Jan Swartz, Nancy Knauff, Ruth Schmuff, Margaret Rhiel, and Phyllis Newman. Nancy Howard's horticulture advice was invauluable and most graciously given when I requested her help. What fabulous friends!

To the suppliers at the Pennock Company, Calvert Wholesale, Massoni Wholesale, and Robin Newman's Company, I am most grateful for up-to-the-minute notification on new materials from the supply departments, as well as obtaining for me the very freshest flowers. Everyone has been so helpful.

But I could not have done any of this without Dr. Mary Betty Stevens. Dr. Alfred Kronthal, and Dr. Douglas Jabs. To them I will always be eternally grateful.

I deeply appreciate the encouragement of my family and my two business partners, Ruth Towlen and Sheila Hyatt, who have lived this book with me every single day. Thanks also to Carol Geist for her marvelous drawings and to our photographer Ken Hostetter for capturing Christmas, and especially for the patience and help from Ellie Heldrich who provided the pinecone bunny and deer and without whom there would be no book. Thank you all for being there for me. Your support has been overwhelming!

IN THE BEGINNING

Designing for Christmas evolved from an interest in Christmas decorations over a period of many years. Some of the ideas presented here are ones I have developed, some are adapted and embellished from things I have seen, some I have been taught by others. Over a period of thirty-some years I have clipped articles from magazines and newspapers and studied them. Few of them had satisfactory instructions for exactly how to begin and complete projects. Mechanics have changed over this period of time, and designs are easier to execute with the advent of Oasis, the hot-glue gun, and various other aids. Remembering back, I think about struggling over my creations for lack of information. I hope these pages will be of assistance to you as you create your individual designs. Since this book is devoted to those just beginning the art of Christmas design, I have used materials widely available and flowers which are standard. Naturally these may be changed, for the most part, to suit the individual arranger. The instructions in this book do not necessarily meet the qualifications necessary for exhibiting in flower shows. You must always check the schedule for special rules when exhibiting.

This book is intended primarily for home use, but whenever you create a decoration it should have a good, firm foundation or it will fall apart, resulting in much disappointment. The mechanics are the most important part of any design. This is what I first teach my classes of novices. It really does pay to purchase the right mechanics for each creation. Many are re-usable, others are not. Never try to re-use Oasis. It will NOT work!

Basically, I am suggesting ideas. Each of you will execute a project differently to make it uniquely your own by your choice of materials and trim. I have a few requests. Be kind to the environment by using sprays only minimally; most paint can be applied by brushing or dipping. Recycle whatever and whenever you can. Cut only living plants that are not on the endangered species list. Try not to cut excess material of any kind.

I do hope you will enjoy designing for Christmas in your own home. Try a few projects you have never tried before, and have patience. I have always lived by the theory, "Everything is impossible for those who never try anything," so I will attempt projects I am not always certain will be successful. Usually they turn out well, giving great pleasure.

I wish you fun and excitement with your decorating in this bright and cheerful time of year.

Best wishes for a Merry Christmas!

Carroll H. Swann

FRESH FRUIT COMPOTE

A selection of fruit is heaped into a compote. The fruit is held in place with Cling floral clay or Oasis double-faced tape, both of which need to be applied to dry fruit at room temperature. After the fruit is arranged to satisfaction, a little water mixed with one egg white is applied selectively with a pastry brush. Granulated sugar is sprinkled over the egg white while it is stlll wet. Afterward the fruit can be eaten.

MECHANICS AND SUPPLIES

When I first began flower arranging, the terminology was baffling at times. My mother used something called a frog to hold flowers in place, and frogs are still in use for certain types of arranging; but floral foam, pinholders, and pincups have replaced them almost entirely. The mechanics of flower design are most important. The successful outcome of an arrangement depends upon a sturdy support system, so select carefully. New floral aids are always coming on the market; below are the ones I know and find most useful. Not all of them were used to create the designs in this book, but you will certainly find all of them useful.

Frog

Frog - A heavy round piece of glass pierced through with holes to accommodate the stems of flowers. A frog is unobtrusive in the bottom of a glass container. Even though some of the holes are at an angle, they hold the stems very straight so there is not much allowance for positioning. I use frogs for very sparse designs with stems that do not fit easily onto a pinholder, such as a few daffodils with a single budding branch. Frogs, used in clear glass containers, should be fixed in place with adhesive and concealed with clear marbles, pebbles, or attractive leaves, such as ivy or myrtle.

Pinholders

Pinholder - A heavy metal item, also called a needlepoint holder, that is made in assorted shapes—round, oval, square, rectangular, and triangular —covered with small spikes or pins which are very sharp. They are ideal to use in shallow bowls that require low, but sturdy, mechanics. Branches pushed down onto the points are held in place very well. Pinholders can be purchased which fit together to form almost any desired shape.

Pincup

Pincup - A metal container which has a pinholder imbedded permanently inside. Pincups are practical where an actual container is not necessary or will not fit, yet a source of water is needed, such as on a very narrow shelf or mantelpiece. They are especially useful inside bowls that may be cracked or on a flat tray-type container. I often use leaves or moss to cover pincups. Pebbles or marbles may be heaped around them.

Floral foam - A kind of plastic foam that will absorb water. There are two types; instant, which fills with water rapidly; and regular which must be allowed to soak for a longer time before it is completely saturated. Submerge both types until no bubbles are seen rising to the surface of the water. Foam comes in different brands, but I recommend Oasis because it holds plant material well and it is available in such a wide variety of shapes and sizes. Floral foam can be trimmed to any shape with a knife. The Deluxe variety of Oasis can be used for large arrangements with heavy-stemmed flowers such as gladioli or birds-of-paradise. Another type of Oasis, called Springtime was created for fragile stems. Sahara is brown foam for silk and dried materials.

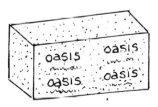

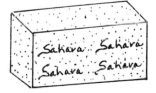

Floral Foam

Cage - A snap-together plastic basket used to hold wet floral foam for foliage or floral designs not supported in a container. There are several different kinds. I often use one of the commercial varieties made by Oasis,

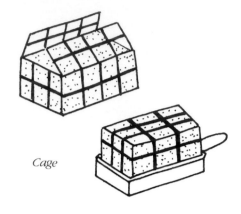

Cage

Iglu

O'Dapter

Racquettes Holder

Mini-deco Holder

Floral Foam Spike

such as their Corso holder or their Place-it holder. Floracage is the name of another product. Floracage Grande is a larger version of Floracage. After a cage has been used, the old floral foam can be removed and replaced with fresh foam for the next arrangement. Cages are an investment well worth making. They can also be filled with Sahara for use with dried or silk material. Cages can be wired into place or they can be attached to flat surfaces with adhesive. They can even be attached to one another. If you do not have access to these commercial products, cages can be created from chicken wire or by filling two plastic berry boxes with wet floral foam and wiring them together to create a single cage.

Iglu - A dome-shaped cage of plastic, made by Oasis, incorporating a removable round disc in the bottom. Iglus can be used separately or they can be wired together to form a larger base to hold flowers or foliage. An Iglu can be nailed to a surface through the side tabs of the cage or it can have the disc removed from the bottom and be pushed down over a tall candle so the base of the candle can wear a ruffle of greens or flowers.

O'dapter - A wonderful invention to hold Oasis for use with candle-sticks and candelabra. The bottom of it fits into the socket of a candle-stick so the Oasis can hold flowers and foliage, or even a candle. After use, discard the foam, but keep the O'dapter to be refilled and used again. Filled with Sahara, an O'dapter can be used for dried or silk flowers.

Raquettes holder - A long rectangular holder, 18″ or 27″, for holding very long designs. It has a perforated, non-removable clear poly covering which allows the Oasis inside to take up water, yet prevents moisture from escaping. Since it has a rigid plastic bottom, it can stand alone.

Mini-deco holders - Oasis makes a small round plastic disc with an adhesive backing, topped with a dome of Oasis. These can be dampened by holding the foam part of the holder upside down in water until the Oasis is thoroughly wet. Do not immerse the whole thing because the backing should not get wet. These are particularly useful for arrangements of tiny flowers and greens to decorate napkin rings, serving platters, presents, or any little place that needs an unexpected touch of color.

Floral foam spike - A small round plastic disc with four prongs used to hold Oasis or Sahara in containers. Spikes can be hot-glued into place for use with dried or silk flowers, or attached with adhesive clay for fresh flower work. They are also called Anchor Pins.

Floral tape - A stretchable waxy tape that is available in many colors. The tape will stick to itself. Use it to attach wires to the stems of flowers and foliage. It is indispensable for corsage work, garlands, and bouquets to cover wires and give a finished natural appearance. Use green with flower stems, brown for pinecones and dried work, natural with light-colored dried materials, white with bleached or painted objects, and black for very dramatic black-background items.

Cling - White or green floral clay used to attach mechanics to containers

or to attach sheets of styrofoam to each other. It is packaged in a long roll with the clay resting on a ribbon of coated paper. You will discover many uses for it when you have it on hand. I do not use it to anchor Sahara or Oasis.

Candleholder - A green plastic holder that has a spike bottom to insert into wet floral foam. It is used to hold candles firmly in floral foam among fresh material. Trying to use a candle in an arrangement without it only creates a large unstable hole in the foam—the candle will never stand straight and inserting other material immediately next to the candle becomes impossible. Candleholders are re-usable.

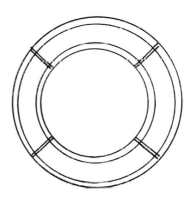

Candleholder

Tall Candleholder

Tall candleholder - A tall version of candleholder set on long plastic legs which allows the use of candles among tall fresh greens and flowers. The one I use is made by Lomey.

Oasis adhesive tapes

Clear - A water-resistant transparent adhesive tape. I use it to create a grid on the top of a clear container so flowers can be supported without the use of other mechanics. It is almost invisible and is easily covered by the fresh materials being used. I also use it to make a single, but smaller, opening in a very large container. This is particularly useful when working with a few tall flowers in a wide-mouth container where the flowers would otherwise fall to one side. A grid of this type allows the materials to be held in the middle of the vase.

Green - Green floral adhesive tape is available in different widths. It can easily be split into thinner strips so you only need to buy the wide width. This is the tape I use most often for fresh designs; for instance, it will hold a large chunk of Oasis upright on a plate for a boxwood tree when used according to the directions on page 50.

Double-faced mounting tape - has adhesive on both sides. It will hold just about anything if it is applied to dry surfaces. After it is in place, it will withstand moisture, but it cannot be attached to a wet or cold surface.

Oasis Wreath Form

Wreath form - A green plastic wreath-frame fitted with Oasis. This is a new item for the Oasis company. A cage of ribs holds the Oasis firmly in place, but the ribs can be detached so the used Oasis can be removed and subsequently replaced. A variation of this is a set of wreath forms called a Ring-Set Holder, which consists of three rings with a round piece in the center—each ring of floral foam has its own plastic base. The ring diameters are 12", 8 1/2", 5 1/2", with a 3 1/4" center pad, none of which can be used more than once.

Pew marker - A sturdy plastic hanger fitted with a cage to hold flowers over the end of a church pew. It will also fit over a fence, banister, gate, or anywhere else you may not want to nail mechanics in place. If you have tie-back draperies held in place by a permanent brass fixture, pew markers can be hung over the fixture and greens can be arranged to enhance the tie-back. I use one made by Lomey.

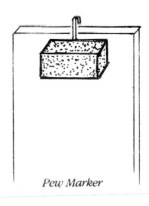

Pew Marker

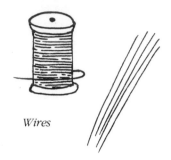

Wires

Wire Clippers

Flower Clippers

Fern Pin

Marbles

Crystals

Pebbles

Small pew marker - A much smaller pew marker by Dakota Plastics. This one can be used over mirrors and the like, wherever you would like to have an arrangement and cannot attach other mechanics.

Wires - I use 18″ long, 18-gauge (#18) wire for most of the things I do. These long, straight wires are very strong, yet can be bent into fern pins, if needed. They are good to use for reinforcing stems of woody branches, but not good for soft flower stems unless they are inserted into the stem. Fine wire—#26, #28, and #30—is used for wiring flower heads and wrapping materials onto a wreath. When extensive wiring is to be done, use wire on a roll instead of the individual straight-length wires. Floral wire ranges in strength from #30, very fine, to #16, very strong.

Wire clippers - Pointed-end clippers of heavy-duty construction. They can be used to cut most types of wires.

Flower clippers - Many varieties are available, but I use a scissors-type preferred for Oriental arranging. They are very sharp and will cut even heavy stems evenly and cleanly. The Snap-Cut brand of clippers, which works with a spring and has a distinctive orange handle, is another favorite of mine.

Fern pin - A strong heavy wire, crimped in the center and bent into a U-shape. They are very useful for securing materials to wreath bases and styrofoam. Also called filly fern pins, S-type fern pins, and greening pins.

Marbles - Small clear glass balls used to cover mechanics in open containers. They are available also in a flattened form that is very attractive to use in special situations. When scattered across the inside of a low bowl, they give the illusion of drops of water even if there is no water in the container. To camouflage pincups and clay, marbles can be imbedded in the clay holding a pincup to a container. This will require fewer marbles than piling them around the pincup. I am not wild about colored marbles, but they are available. Black marbles are good to use with contemporary or Oriental work, but they are very shiny and could become more of a feature than a mechanic.

Crystals - Glass chips, treated so they will not cut your hands. They give the illusion of crushed ice and make great cover-ups for mechanics. I use only the clear variety, but colors are available. Personally, I feel colors are distracting when used inside a crystal vase.

Pebbles - an Oriental variety of polished, rounded, dark stones. They come in black, charcoal, brown, white, and mottled. River gravel is often used in naturalistic designs. I do not use white crusher-run stones because they have a powdery residue that clouds the water. Any pebbles used in a flower design should be perfectly clean.

Mosses - Natural materials used for covering mechanics and filling holes. Sheet moss is the most commonly used moss for floral work. It is available dried and can be somewhat revitalized by being soaked in water. Do not,

CRYSTAL TREES CENTERPIECE

A mirror underneath is important to achieve an icy look from these trees. Rock candy or clear glass chips are glued onto white styrofoam cones with hot glue. Begin at the bottom of the cone, applying hot glue in small sections and quickly press the crystals into the glue. The hot glue will melt some of the styrofoam but not enough to cause problems. The work does not need to be completed at a single sitting. If you use rock candy, some of the large pieces may need to be broken, a few at time, by putting them in a plastic bag and striking them with a hammer. Rock candy makes a more opaque tree than glass crystals, but the candy is less expensive and easier to work with.

Chenille Stems

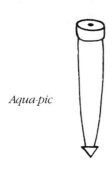

Aqua-pic

Orchid Vial

Grid

however, use it in a clear vase full of water as it will shed and discolor the water. Sphagnum moss is a fuller type of dried moss which also sheds. I use quantities of both sphagnum and sheet moss during the Christmas season to make natural-looking bases for some of my work. Deer moss is silvery-gray in color, becomes spongelike in water and, when dry, is quite hard. To fill open spaces in dried work, it is inserted while wet and allowed to dry to fit the space. Spanish moss is also silvery-gray in color and comes in long strands. When used damp it is very soft and pretty, but when dry it becomes rather messy, dropping little bits and pieces. An imitation moss is also available that comes on a plastic sheet. It is dark green and fairly believable if used with subtlety. I only use it inside openwork baskets which must last a long time.

Chenille stems - Extra-fuzzy pipe cleaners that come in white or green to use with fresh materials. They allow moisture to reach the flower heads when they are inserted inside hollow stems. They can also be used to wire fragile flower heads, such as small orchids that would otherwise be damaged by uncovered wires.

Aqua-pics - Green plastic vials with snap-on rubber covers, perforated with a single hole, and pointed ends. The vials hold water for flowers which otherwise would have no source of moisture, and the points allow them to be inserted into dirt, foam, fruit arrangements, or onto branches. Aqua-pics come in several different lengths and can be attached to very long, sturdy wires to give additional length to flowers with short stems used in very large, full arrangements.

Orchid vials - Small clear tubes used for orchids when they are being shipped to market. I use them to supply water for very small flowers used with non-living materials. They have a snap-on cap with a small hole for the flower stem. Wonderful to use for inserting pieces of cut vines into fruit arrangements.

Grid - A round circle of plastic, cut like a grating, which can be placed over the top of a glass container for the purpose of arranging flowers without the use of inside mechanics. Made by Brady Grid-Locks.

Liner - any secondary watertight container that is placed inside another container to hold water. Containers are necessary for baskets, cracked or porous pottery containers, or to protect delicate or valuable containers from coming into contact with flower water. Some containers come with liners; but for others, such things as margarine tubs, jars, cookware, or deli salad containers will work.

Paint - available in many varieties and colors for different purposes. Because I disapprove the use of spray paints that are harmful to our atmosphere, here is a list of the alternative products I am learning how to use. Meanwhile, for decorations used at Christmas, I have discovered that certain brands offer better colors than others. For gold, I use a gold leaf paint made for frames and furniture trim by UGL. It comes in a small jar and produces a very bright gold color. Art stores frequently have fine quality paints in cans, and I often use liquid shoe polish to deepen the color of wood. Not all paints can be used on candles or styrofoam. Check labels and read all the precautions. The paint I use to paint plywood forms is Martin-Senour's Great Life Experience latex satin-gloss house paint in Shutter Green. It produces a color that blends well with evergreens. So many products are available already dyed or painted that I try to purchase already finished materials. According to manufacturers, spray paints by Design Master and Perfect Touch contain no fluoro-carbons and are environmentally safe.

Glue gun - A hand-held electric tool filled with glue that can be applied in a hot stream wherever it is wanted by a pull of the trigger. THE GLUE IS VERY HOT AND CAN CAUSE BURNS! After being burned several times, I developed a healthy respect for this gadget, using the trigger with a light hand and always keeping a cold, wet sponge beside me to touch a burn immediately. Extra-long glue sticks are available for doing a large amount of gluing at one time. Hot glue may be removed from an object to which it has been applied by heating it with warm air from a hair dryer.

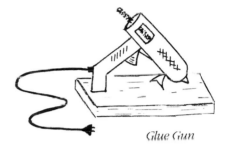

Glue Gun

Floral pick - A sliver of dark green wood, quite sturdy, with one end pointed and a fine wire attached to the opposite end. Picks are available in several different lengths and are used to attach fresh and dried materials to their base mechanics.

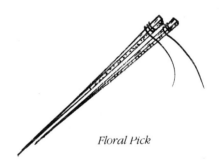

Floral Pick

Hillman handi-wreath frame - A ring of wire with short cross wires welded on at regular intervals. Small boughs of bushy evergreens can easily be made into a wreath if laid on the ring and held in place by the bendable arms.

Wreath hanger - A simple solution to the problem of how to hang a wreath on a glass door is the wreath hanger. Using a sturdy grade of sheet metal, cut a 3″ wide strip about 18″ long. Bend one end of the strip to fit over the top of the door. Bend the other end up to form a hanger to hold the wreath. The hanger then becomes an integral part of your design and may be painted or covered with ribbon.

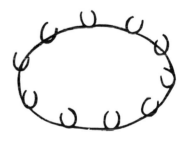

Hillman Handi-wreath Frame

Wreath Hanger

RIBBONS

Most ribbons come in several widths and colors so there are many from which to choose. Some lace or velvet ribbons can be cut to a narrower width, but cotton and satin will unravel if you try to split them.

Ribbons are most often used singly, but combinations of ribbons are very effective. When using a narrow ribbon over a wider one, keep the top ribbon centered. If you have difficulty keeping the two ribbons together, use tiny pieces of double-stick adhesive tape. When combining ribbons keep in mind that the heavier weight fabric should be on the bottom. Choose materials appropriate to the type of home you have.

To decide what width ribbon to use, let proportion be the guide. Most large wreaths, 14" or more in diameter, require a 3" ribbon to be in scale with the size and visual weight of the decoration; however, a 3" ribbon would probably be too wide for a wall sconce. Ribbons, like the decorations themselves, must be in harmony and scale with their surroundings.

The following list of ribbons and their uses is based on many years of experience working with ribbons and bows. New products are always coming on the market, so be open to experimentation.

Velvet ribbons have a very rich appearance. There are two types: one for inside use, and one which is weather-resistant. Velvet tubing is marvelous for use as a round, thin streamer. It is easy to tie into a soft loose bow, but humidity will make it droop.

Bright colored **yarn** is attractive for whimsical wreaths or for wreaths decorated in a Mexican, Southwestern, or Scandinavian motif.

Plastic ribbons are the only ribbons that are truly water resistant; but unless you live in an area which is constantly deluged with downpours of rain, please do not use them. They do not have the quality usually associated with a private home.

Imitation satin ribbons have a very sleek, smooth surface and they hold their shape well. They have more body than the more expensive pure satin ribbons. True satin ribbon is luxurious, usually finished with a high-quality edging, and has a very opulent aura. Soft and flowing, it is intended for indoor use, and nothing can surpass it for beauty.

The new **paper** ribbons are fun and interesting to use. They are fairly strong, resist tearing, and hold their shape well. They are intended for indoor use, as dampness and paper do not mix. Paper ribbons are ideal for informal country style.

Raffia is charming and comes in very thin strips which can be gathered together for fullness. It is a pliable straw-like material which is useful for both natural and country-style wreaths. Raffia will tolerate a certain amount of dampness; but if it becomes wet, it will be limp.

Cotton ribbon comes in many different patterns and colors, but the patterns are not usually printed on both sides. I use it with another ribbon, usually imitation satin, underneath, working the two together, so the unfinished side will not show. The underlying ribbon helps give the cotton ribbon extra body. Do not use cotton ribbons outside.

Moiré ribbon is very elegant, holds its shape, has a lustrous finish, and is for inside use; unless you can find one which has been treated for outside use.

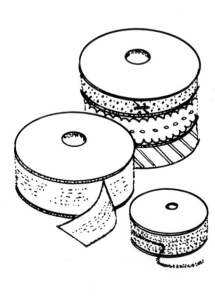

These gift boxes with big bows show how to wrap a box so the ribbon is not disturbed when the box is opened.

Burlap ribbon is rustic and sturdy and comes in many colors. I have used it outside under cover of a roof. However, it will not withstand high humidity or direct water showers.

Metallic ribbon is a favorite at Christmas because it catches the light and glimmers with reflections. There are several types available. One I like to use has an almost mirror finish and is quite stiff. It can be used outside. A bow made from this ribbon can be stored away with other ornaments and brought out again the following year. It is appropriate with greens and glistening ornaments. A softer-looking woven metallic ribbon, called **lamé,** is wonderful for draping and to weave through sprays of greens. A stiff variety of woven metallic ribbon can be used outside.

Lace ribbon is very soft and delicate. It is intended for inside use, but I have used it over velvet ribbon outside under cover with no harmful effect. When used over velvet or satin it has a Victorian flavor.

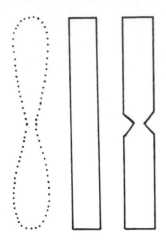

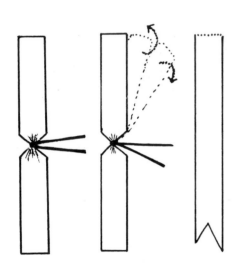

BOW MAKING

Here is the simplest way I have ever found to make a bow for a wreath or package.

To make a bow for a wreath on a standard-size door, use ribbon about 3″ wide. Take the end of a spool of ribbon and bend it over on itself to form a loop 10 1/2″ to 11″ long. Hold the cut end of the ribbon in place and wrap the spool end around the cut end and up the other way to form a second loop around the first one. Repeat wrapping the ribbon over and over ten times until there are many loops on top of each other. Hold the loops together neatly with their edges in alignment. The result should be a tightly constructed figure 8 of ribbon held in the middle by your hand. After the tenth loop, cut the ribbon from the spool, making the cut even with the end of the loops.

Still holding the looped ribbon together in the middle, fold it in half to find the exact center. Open it back out and cut a small V in each side of the ribbon. Do not let the V cuts touch each other. There must be an uncut bridge in the middle so the bow does not fall apart.

Take an 18″ length of narrow ribbon in the same color as the bow and tie it securely into a knot where the cuts were made. This could be a 1/2″ width of ribbon slit from ribbon remaining on the spool.

Holding the top half of the figure 8 securely in one hand, gently but firmly pull out each loop from the inside, giving it a little twist to secure it in place. Alternate pulling the loops to the front and the back. Turn and repeat the same process on the other end. With all the loops pulled out, the result should be a round, puffy bow.

If you want streamers to flow from the bow, cut a length of the same ribbon two times the desired finished length. Fold the streamer ribbon in half and cut a small V on each side of the center fold. Place the streamers behind the finished bow and secure them to the bow with the same narrow ribbon, still attached, used to tie the bow together. Cut the ends of the streamers at angles so they are not both the same length. Streamers can be woven through the greens of a wreath or swag.

Bows from different widths of ribbon should be different sizes. So your bows will be well-proportioned, here are the correct loop lengths for the different widths of standard ribbon.

Width of Ribbon	Length of Loop
1/2″	4 1/2″ to 5″
1″	5 1/2″
1 1/2″	6″
2 1/4″	8″ to 8 1/2″
2 1/2″	9″ to 10″
2 3/4″ to 3″	10 1/2″ to 11″

The narrower ribbons may need more loops for a full bow. Try 12 to 15 loops for the 1 1/2″ wide ribbon.

FRESH FLOWERS AND FOLIAGE

Without being technical horticulturally, I find that evergreens fall into two categories: the broadleaf variety, and the needled variety. An evergreen is a plant—perennial, tree, or shrub—that remains green throughout the year. They usually grow new leaves or needles before shedding their old ones. Some evergreen foliage remains on the tree for several years. Some evergreens produce cones, some produce berries, and some even have decorative flowers. Most are long lasting when cut for foliage, especially if soaked in water overnight.

Cedar

Try to use a mixture of different evergreens together in an arrangement. Cedar has a delightful aroma. Blue spruce has beautiful blue-green foliage. The long-needled pines are particularly useful for arranging because a handful of them, removed from the branch, can be bound together and taped onto a stiff wire to be inserted for height or width in a design. Juniper produces lovely blue-gray berries.

Holly is invaluable at Christmas. It is probably the most familiar of the broadleafed plants, having nearly 300 species. English holly is a very deep green in color and usually has an abundance of berries. Variegated hollies are good for accent touches and centers of interest. Not all hollies have red berries. Some have yellow; my Burford holly has peachy-orange berries. These are useful for those who don't want red. Mahonia, or Oregon grape holly, has leaves that are almost slate-green in color. Pittisporum has leaves that grow in a whorl-shaped pattern; it is available in solid green as well as variegated.

English Holly

Boxwood and privet are great fillers for designs. Magnolia grandiflora leaves are large and handsome to use not only as background for other materials, but also as a focal point. Pyracantha and cotoneaster have slender branches used to achieve height and line, especially useful in comtemporary designs.

In most parts of this country, fresh garden flowers are not available in December, so they must be purchased for Christmas arrangements. Therefore, most flowers have already been conditioned by the florist when you get them. Still, it is a good practice to re-cut the stems with a sharp knife and place them in a bucket of lukewarm water for several hours. The florist may provide a packet of preservative to add to the water. It will help prolong the life of the flowers. A little sugar added to the water is a good substitute.

Magnolia

When buying flowers, check the stems and leaves to see if the flowers are fresh. The lower leaves especially may be yellow and tired. The stems should look crisp and the leaves green and sturdy. Carnation flowers should not be fully open. They should have a well-rounded head and the outer petals should not be drooping. Freesia florets should be standing straight on their stems, with no tiny brown lines showing. Roses should be in the process of opening, not fully opened when you buy them. A few of the outside rose petals may need to be removed, but that is of no consequence. Buy flowers in the tight stage a day or two before you plan to use them. Keep them cold until you are ready for them to open.

White Pine

If the flowers are in a vase, the water should be changed daily to prolong their life.

ALL GREEN ARRANGEMENT

A gathering of greens from the garden, with as many different varities as possible, becomes impressive in a handsome container. For a foc point, add pinecones, interesting pods, and berried branches. Arrangments of greens do not need flowers or ornaments. The material with t greatest visual weight should be placed toward the bottom, mediu weight greens and lighter, lacy materials can be used throughout. Fo full, lush effect, the design should be finished all the way around, even i will only be seen from one side.

DRIED AND CONTRIVED MATERIALS

Dried materials with unique shapes can add distinctive touches to an arrangement. Many can be painted to add a splash of color to an arrangement of Christmas greens. Others can give added height for a tall design. They can be saved from year to year, and a new coat of paint will make them fresh again.

Some materials grow naturally and some are contrived and manufactured, such as the curly rattan spirals. Often in design work there is need for a certain shape which is not available, so a new "pod" is born.

For over-size arrangements, there are some very tall materials available. For instance, Unryu Yanagi is a tall twisted stick, usually 36" to 48" in height. Mitsumata is another. These are superlative to achieve height in floor designs.

The advantage of using dried and preserved materials for Christmas decorations is that they do not need water and will look just as fresh at the end of the holiday as they did in the beginning. With care, they can even be used another season.

Feathers and gourds are among the unusual materials I like to use at Christmas. Pheasant feathers, available from florist and craft shops, are outstanding when used with vine wreaths. They add a masculine flavor to certain settings, and make a perfect accent with dried materials for an apartment door. Gourds come in interesting sizes, textures, and shapes and they can be painted in metallic colors to add to an arrangement of greens. They are difficult to penetrate for the purpose of securing them to wires or picks with anything less than a hammer and nail or an electric drill. Because they are not expensive, they are ideal to use for outside decorations.

I dry some material myself by hanging it, using silica gel, or treating it with glycerine and water. It takes time for flowers to dry, often a week or more. Gather them on a dry day at the height of their season. Flowers such as Queen Anne's lace, growing along roadways during the summer, are lovely dried by the silica gel method for use at Christmas. Roses, dried by hanging, take about ten days. When roses dry they shrink considerably, so dry more than you think you will use.

Press ferns and other foliage between two sheets of paper towelling and insert them in the pages of a book. Weight the book with a heavy object or another large book and leave the preserving in the hands of time. Preserved leaves are invaluable for dried arrangements because dried materials have little or no foliage of their own.

Glycerinized materials last well and are not as fragile as materials dried by other methods, but they frequently become darker in color. Baby's breath, for instance, becomes tan; and eucalyptus becomes dark blue. Magnolia and beech leaves are worth glycerinizing at home because they are not currently available commercially.

Glycerinizing must be done during the growing season when the plant material is able to absorb moisture. To glycerinize magnolia and beech branches, mix one part glycerine and two parts hot water in a container. Stir well. I use an electric blender to mix mine thoroughly. Cut the stems at a sharp angle and hammer the ends so they split. This enables them to soak up more of the mixture. Place branches into a container

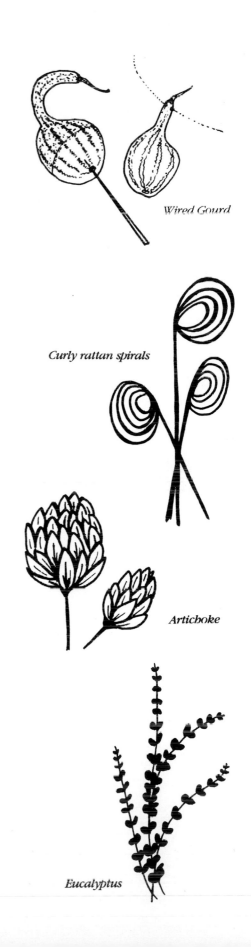

Wired Gourd

Curly rattan spirals

Artichoke

Eucalyptus

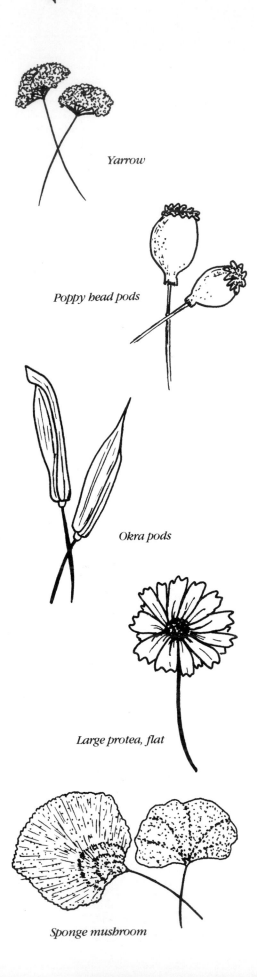

Yarrow

Poppy head pods

Okra pods

Large protea, flat

Sponge mushroom

filled at least four inches high with the solution. Leave the container in a cool, dark place for about 10 days to allow for complete absorption of the solution. It is completely preserved when small drops of glycerine begin to appear on the leaves, or when the leaves have become a deeper color. Remove the branches from the solution and wash them thoroughly.

Individual leaves can be glycerinized by submerging them in a fifty-fifty solution of hot water and glycerine. After 6 or 7 days, remove the leaves and wash off the excess solution. Dry them with paper towels. Stems may be added to glycerinized leaves by taping them to sturdy #18 florist wires with floral tape, or wiring them to floral picks. The deep rich colors of glycerinzed leaves are handsome to use with pheasant feathers, pinecones and pods, or even alone in an attractive container.

Freeze-dried flowers have become available commercially. They are said to resemble fresh flowers. The petals of roses, for instance are quite pliable, but they look shiny and slippery. The bloom does not shrink as much as a dried flower nor is it as perishable, but neither does it look fresh.

Most dried materials can be used with fresh materials as long as they do not come in contact with water. The stems should be wrapped with florist tape and secured to wires or a wooden pick before they are inserted into wet floral foam. Baby's breath, of course, can just be placed into a design where it will be held in place by the surrounding materials.

I have discovered it is possible to revitalize many dried flowers that look a little wrinkled and drawn by briefly holding them over a steaming teapot, then carefully smoothing out their petals. They need to dry again for an hour or so after this treatment.

Purchased dried materials usually come ready-to-use with their stems finished neatly, but if you buy pods on wires, for a professional-looking finish, the wires will need to be wrapped with floral tape in colors to match the materials of the design.

Pinecones rarely come ready-to-use. Often they must be baked in a 250° oven for 30 minutes so they open completely, and to kill any insects. To prepare a pinecone for use in a design, wrap a wire around the lower scales, twist together, and attach the cone to a wooden pick with the wire.

The cones of the longleaf pine are quite large, ranging from 6″ to 10″ in length and, when fully open, they make a handsome display. The sugar pine produces the largest cones—up to two feet in length—so large they can be turned into little Christmas trees all by themselves by standing them upright on a base and decorating their scales with little ornaments. The Western white pine also produces a very long cone, wonderful in horizontal designs requiring length. For small, round, flat cones, look for the Scotch pine, Austrian pine, or black pine. Very large cones are produced by hemlocks, redwoods, and cedar.

Long pinecones, such as spruce and white pine, may be split in half. To do this, make a cut at the bottom of the cone with clippers. After the cone has been split a portion of the way up, it can usually be pulled apart. Long cones can also be cut crosswise into rounds that look a little like flowers. The slices can be wired or glued into place. Slices of pinecone are particularly pretty massed in a garland.

Cones can be taken apart scale by scale and the scales used individually. Large scales can be wired through a hole punched in the bottom and used on long stems in designs, or they can be glued onto plastic or papermaché animal shapes one by one to create scale-covered woodland birds or animals. There are a few tricks to this: the scales should be glued on so they are all going in the same direction—the way the fur or feathers naturally lie, they should follow the lines of the molded base, and individual scales can be trimmed with scissors. Mixing scales from various types of cones can change color and texture.

Curling, twisting vines and branches lend themselves to many designs using fresh, dried, or artificial materials. They provide a feeling of controlled disorder, of wild and natural beauty. Grapevines are popular, but many other vines are attractive and plentiful, also. Wisteria, bittersweet, Harry Lauder's walking stick, fasciated willow, and curly willow are a few I have used. Cut these materials in the green stage. Before they dry, bend and wrap them into whatever shape or position is desired, and wire them in place. They will dry in the shape you give them.

The color of vines may be changed by applying liquid shoe polish or paint, but vines are always appropriate in their natural color. They give any design life and movement.

Look along roadsides when the leaves are falling to find the perfect vine for any arrangement. Honeysuckle is a great find for an arranger. A walk in a forest may yield a graceful branch or vine. Spare the tiny tendrils. They add charm to a design. The more unusual the material, the more interesting the design. Gather anything interesting.

Baby's breath is a flower that is available in several conditions—fresh, natural, preserved, bleached and preserved, and glittered.

Fresh baby's breath will dry naturally in place. Baskets full of it have an airy appearance, but it will shrink as it dries. The plant has a strange smell when it is drying so you may prefer to let it dry in the garage or basement for a few days before introducing it to the living room.

Natural dried baby's breath, bought from the florist, should be sprayed with warm water before use. This helps reduce the loss of blossoms as florets are being pulled from the bunch.

Preserved baby's breath has a tan cast and is an excellent filler with dried materials.

Bleached and preserved baby's breath is very white and unsurpassed for Christmas designs with painted or bleached materials. It handles well, keeps its color, and does not shed heavily. Glittered professionally, it is wonderful to use in arrangements of evergreens and ornaments.

Hydrangeas are becoming one of the most popular flowers used for decorating. Cut them in the summer when they are at their peak, and hang them upside down to dry in a dark, dry place. Small florets can be dried in silica-gel to fill small spaces or for use in tiny designs.

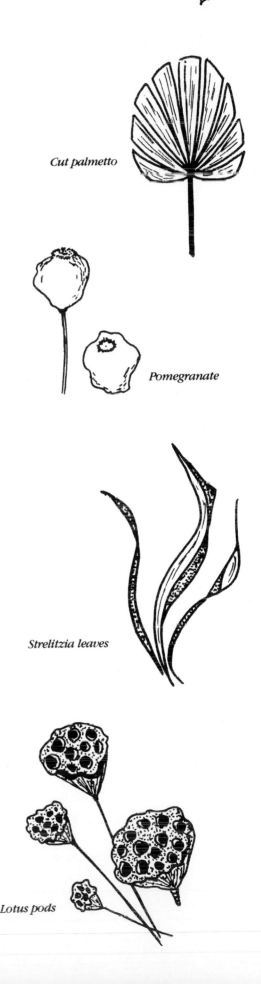

Cut palmetto

Pomegranate

Strelitzia leaves

Lotus pods

FLOOR-STANDING DRIED ARRANGEMENT

Designed for a contemporary setting, this arrangement of dried, contrived, and artificial materials is built on a block of Sahara wedged into place in the top of a tall glass container. Floral adhesive tape was criss-crossed over the top of the Sahara to hold it in place. Hot glue could have been used to hold the foam. The focal point is an over-size silk flower. Strelitzia and Queen Anne's lace were enhanced with glitter. Palmetto leaves painted black support the line.

DRIED MINI-WREATHS

Standard-size soup can
Spool of medium wire, #22
Spool of fine wire, #30
Sheet moss
Small dried flowers and fern

Hot glue gun
  or
White craft glue
Tweezers
Thin ribbon

Using a soup can as a pattern, wind a length of medium wire from a spool around the can five or six times to form the wreath base. Slip the rounds of wire from the can and wire them together so they do not become separated. The result should be a perfectly round base on which to work.

With fine wire, secure damp sheet moss tightly into place all the way around the wreath, completely covering the wire base. Keep the moss closely cropped or it will become too bushy, defeating the purpose of creating a small wreath. Allow the moss wreath to dry before starting the next step.

Arrange tiny dried flowers and pieces of preserved or dry fern—dried flat under the weight of books—on the wreath base. Use a pair of tweezers to position the flowers and fern. When the effect is pleasing, glue the flowers and leaves into place. I use craft glue with tweezers for this operation, but hot glue will work if you use small drops and watch your fingers! Be sure to finish the sides of the wreath as well as the top, because decorating only the top will result in a flat wreath. Tiny pieces of fresh baby's breath can be added to give the wreath airiness and fullness. Finish the wreath by adding a loop of narrow ribbon by which it can be hung. Additional bows of the same ribbon can be glued in place, if you wish.

A similar version of this wreath can be made by using the same moss-covered base and covering the moss completely with white statice or baby's breath. This will become a white background wreath instead of a wreath with a green background. It will also make the wreath rather plump, and the hole in the middle will be much smaller. The scale of any added flowers can be just a bit larger because the overall wreath will be larger. Very small jewelry-type beads can be glued into the statice for a more sophisticated wreath.

These are wonderful little decorations to hang in a small spot, or to give as gifts. If you dry flowers from your garden to use for decorating, include some small flowers to press or dry with silica gel so you can make some of these wreaths. This makes the gift of a wreath even more precious to one who receives it as a present. Don't overlook individual florets from larger flowers such as hydrangeas. Dry things as they come into season and store them away carefully until needed.

These small wreaths last a long, long time. After the Christmas season, wrap each wreath in tissue paper and place in a plastic bag until next year. I have used mine successfully for over five years.

A WELCOMING ENTRANCE

The ways you can welcome family and friends to your house during the Christmas season will depend upon the design of your house and landscape. **Rural route mailboxes** are a delight to see all trimmed for Christmas. The Post Office does not object to the trimming of standard mailboxes for this short season as long as nothing interferes with the opening and closing of the box. A swag of greens placed on the top, a garland wrapped around the post, a big bow with a cluster of holly, all say Merry Christmas in the nicest possible way. A long-lasting decoration to consider is the use of painted gourds in the design. Painted with gold or silver paint and wired to a bow, gourds are attractive and inexpensive. They are very hard, however, so a hole for wiring will have to be drilled through them at the stem end.

If you have a **lamppost** lighting the way to your front door, it can be trimmed with a full bow just under the lantern and a wrap of the same ribbon trailing down the post. A few snips of greenery can be added at the bow. For a more elaborate design, the garland can be evergreen. A favorite decoration of mine for the lamppost includes a string of golden bells, made by painting clay pots and hanging them bottom up. The rope used to tie the bells together should be in proportion to the size of the pots. The rope must be able to pass through the drain holes in the bottom of the pots. Make a knot at the end of the rope to resemble a clapper, and pass the other end of the rope up through the pot to emerge from the hole. Inside the pot, mark the place on the rope where it passes through the hole. Tie a second knot at the mark to fit snugly against the hole on the inside to keep the rope from pulling out of the bell. These clay bells in their natural terra cotta color are appropriately rustic used with grapevine and other natural materials. The pots must be the kind that will look like bells when they are hanging.

A decorated **gate** always gives a welcome sign during the holidays. Don't forget to do both sides because a gate will be seen both coming and going. A wrought iron gate offers an easy work surface for attaching material. For a single gate, a wreath, swag, or even ribbons would be attractive. Fix any decoration firmly to the bottom as well as the top if the gate will be in use. If a wreath is being used, hang a similar one on the reverse side so when looking through the posts of the gate, it will appear as one, large, continuous wreath. If you choose not to duplicate your decoration, then at least finish the back of a single wreath so that anything seen through the posts will be attractive when approaching from the other direction.

If you would rather not use greens, make a big bow of red velvet water-resistant ribbon with long streamers falling to the bottom edge of the gate. Fish tail the ends of the ribbon by cutting a V at each end. Repeat on the reverse side of the gate. Wired berries, holly, or unbreakable ornaments tucked into the bow give a holiday accent. Another ribbon decoration would be to trim the gate with a bow attached in the center of a diagonally-placed ribbon.

For double gates decorated with a split wreath, attach the bow to the gate which is secondary—the one which does not move. The moving gate should be free of impediments if possible. When constructing this design, keep the gate closed so the bow will look as if it is attached to both sides.

Wooden post and rail fences often have a wide gate made exactly the same way as the fence itself, which limits creativity. Often garlands wound around the rails or draped generously across the top will do the trick. A wreath placed in the center can offer a focal point.

Wooden privacy fences usually have a gate with a large surface on which to work. You can treat this gate as a wall, with the added advantage of being able to staple, tack, or nail right into it without too much worry. With this kind of gate, you can create almost any display, just as you would on a front door. Remember to affix everything in a sturdy fashion so your work will not be destroyed by the motion of the gate.

If your gate is extremely ornate, keep the trim to a minimum. A center placque, swag, or wreath would be more impressive than too many bows or ornaments.

If you have a favorite **planter or urn** on your porch or entranceway that is used for summer flowers, use it as an outside container for a Christmas gathering of greens, too. Remove the dead and wilted plants of summer and the soil. Place a liner inside the planter and fill it with wet floral foam. Arrange cut greens in the foam to create the effect of plant or bush growing inside the container. When it snows the greens will peek through their cap of white, looking cheerful. Tiny battery-operated lights can be added for use at night. Bright red velvet weather-resistant bows are a colorful option. Pots kept outside during the winter must be able to withstand freezing weather or they will crack and break when moisture inside them freezes and expands.

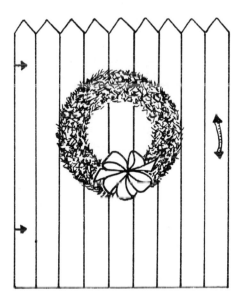

A CRESCENT FOR THE FRONT DOOR

24" wire wreath frame, cut in half
Spool of fine wire
Assorted freshly-cut evergreens
Assorted pods, cones, dried statice,
  and eucalyptus
Two full branches of artificial greens
Wire clippers
Hammer and nails
Bow

This crescent is really quite easy to construct. It looks more difficult than it is. A 24" wreath frame will look too large, but when it is cut in half it will be the right size for a standard-size front door. Use wire clippers to snip the frame in half. Working with one half only, pull the frame out of its semi-circular form into a longer, less round shape—a crescent.

Wire the sprays of artificial greens to the crescent so they fill the inside of the frame. Place one so it is going up toward the top and the other facing toward the bottom. This will become the base on which to work.

Insert sprigs of freshly-cut greens (I used polished variegated holly) along the entire length of the crescent, following the direction of the artificial greens. Make sure the fresh greens are going in the same direction as the artificial material underneath. Fill out the crescent by wiring on cones, pods, holly, and other trims ; and, finally, a bow in the middle where the ends of the greens meet.

It will take three nails to hang this decoration — one in the center of the design, and one on each end. The nails will catch onto the frame under the crescent and hold it securely to the door.

After Christmas, remove only the fresh greens and save the base of artificial greens, pods and cones for the next year.

The remaining half of the wreath frame can be used as the base for a half-circle decoration over a door, or as the base of a second crescent decoration. This design would also be lovely done in dried materials on a moss base, or in cones and pods for an architectural accent.

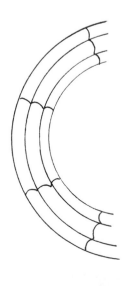

HALF-TOPIARY FOR A DOOR

Half-round wall basket with liner, but no handle
Plaster of Paris
Thick dowel, painted
Two blocks of wet floral foam wrapped in chicken wire
or
Two Iglus
Small nails or wire and adhesive tape
Foil or plastic wrap to cover back of mechanics
Boxwood, amount depends on size of design
Holly and pine sprigs
Moss
Two battery-operated sets of tree lights with green wires
Ribbons
Hook and nail for hanging

Measure the amount of space available for the design on the door and estimate how tall the finished design should be. All other measurements will depend upon the size of the finished design.

The basket is the container in which the design is built; it must be large enough to carry the height and weight of the completed topiary. If you can only find a half-basket with a handle, the handle must be removed, but be careful because some handles are part of the weave and cannot be separated.

Determine what length dowel will be needed for the topiary trunk. Measure the height from the bottom of the inside of the basket to the top of the tree. Cut the dowel and paint or stain it to resemble a tree trunk.

Place the liner in the basket; and, if it wobbles, fix it in place with floral clay. Mix plaster of Paris as the label directs and pour into the liner. Place the painted dowel into the plaster before it starts to harden. The placement of the dowel should be a few inches from the flat back of the basket and centered. This will enable you to achieve a three dimensional effect as you work. If the dowel is too far back in the basket, the design will be too flat when completed. Hold the dowel straight and steady for a few minutes until the plaster sets up. Let the plaster harden for a few hours or overnight before making the rest of the decoration.

Hammer two small nails into opposite sides of the dowel at the place where the bottom of the cage for the lower decorative unit will rest. This will keep the cage from slipping down the dowel. Another way to do this would be to wrap a ridge of wire covered with floral adhesive tape at that same location.

Cut a block of foam into two pieces of slightly different size. Wrap the smaller piece in chicken wire for the bottom decorative unit. Lace the chicken wire together with wire. Cover the back of the cage with aluminum foil or plastic so no moisture will be in contact with the door or wall where the topiary will be used. Slide this cage down the dowel to its chosen location. Or, use an Iglu with its flat side against the wall.

Prepare a restraining mechanic for the top decorative unit with either nails or wire. Wrap the remaining piece of foam in another piece of chicken wire and bind it together with wire. Add the protective foil shield. Slide this second cage over the top of the dowel to its chosen location. Or, use a second Iglu, back against the wall.

Fill the cages of foam, or Iglus, with boxwood so they become full half globes. Check as you work to be sure the tree will rest flat against the

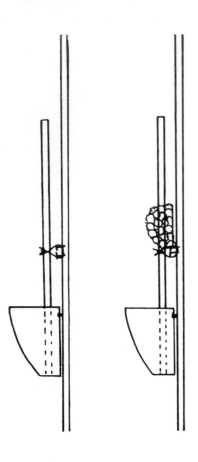

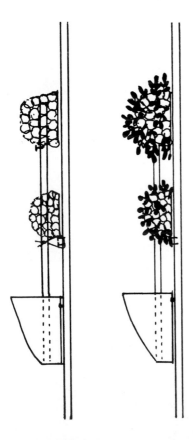

wall. The top unit should be slightly larger than the bottom unit. Cover the cages completely so no mechanics are showing. Be sure to check the bottom! Try for a fully rounded effect. Trim off any excess boxwood to give a neat appearance. There should be some space between the two units. Give the boxwood a quick spray of plant polish from a pump-spray bottle to add luster to the leaves.

At this point it would be a good idea to prepare the hanging mechanics for the tree so the design can be checked in place. Place two nails in the door or wall onto which the basket can be impaled. The nails should be placed on a level line about 1" in from each end of the basket. Hold the basket up to the nails and visually choose a place for two more nails along the line of the dowel, at a spot just above or below the location of the bottom cage. These two nails should be placed on either side of the dowel so a wire can be passed from one to the other across the dowel.

With the topiary in place, make any necessary corrections to the greenery—adding or trimming where necessary for the best effect.

Battery-operated lights can be used to decorate the topiary. Take time to spread the tiny lights evenly throughout each decorative unit. Bulbs may be unscrewed if necessary to balance the placement. The battery pack or packs, depending upon the size of your design, can be hidden in the back of the topiary or in the basket. Additional ornaments and ribbons can be used so the topiary will be pretty in the daytime, too.

Fill the basket with damp moss piled to the rim to cover the plaster of Paris.

EVERGREEN WREATH ON METAL FRAME

Metal wreath frame
Sphagnum moss
Strips of dark green plastic, perhaps
   cut from trash bags, or use
   commercial wreath wrap

Freshly-cut greens
Fern pins
Roll of fine green floral wire
Wooden floral picks with wires
Ribbons, pinecones, and other trims

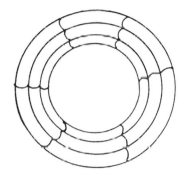

Wire Wreath Frame

Fill the metal wreath frame with packed, wet sphagnum moss. Wrap the wreath completely with strips of plastic until all the moss is covered. Secure the ends of the plastic with fern pins. Cut the chosen greenery into lengths of 6" or 8" with an angled point for easy insertion.

If a wreath is to be used on a door that opens into the house, not out, select materials that do not shed. I like to use Fraser fir because it holds its needles. Boxwood is also an excellent choice. Magnolia leaves are lovely to use over or under other materials. Alone, they make a wreath appear flat. Holly makes a full wreath, but is difficult to insert into the plastic. I use it over other materials as a secondary green.

Fraser Fir

Insert greens, all going in the same direction, through the plastic wrap and into the wet moss. Secure each stem with a fern pin so the material will lie flat against the plastic. Overlap greens so each successive piece is placed under or over the preceding piece. No plastic should be showing. I like to do the inside and outside edges of the wreath first, then the back and, finally, the front. Wrap the wreath with fine wire so the greens do not fall out. The wire will be hidden by the foliage. Excess material can be pruned away.

Attach a piece of wire to the back of the wreath for hanging. To wire a bow to a wreath slip a piece of wire through its back, twisting the wire together leaving two long stems, and work the wires through the greens, twisting them together again in back of the wreath. Wire selected trims to wooden picks and insert the picks into the wreath.

The focal point of a wreath is usually near the bow. It can be on the side, top, or bottom of the wreath. If no bow is used, then a design can be carried completely around the wreath by repeating trim materials, or a ribbon can be woven throughout the entire wreath.

Making a **split wreath** on a metal frame is similar to making a whole wreath except, for double doors or gates, the wreath must open in the middle. Make two frames by cutting a whole frame in half with heavy wire cutters.

Stuff both halves with damp sphagnum moss and wire over the open ends. Wrap both frames with strips of green plastic attaching the beginnings and ends of the plastic with fern pins set at an angle so they will not come out.

Position the undecorated frames on the door where they will be displayed. Determine the location for the hooks or nails to hang the wreath halves and install the hardware. Do some initial greening-in of the frames at your workplace making sure that the greens are inserted as if they were on one single wreath. I suggest you finish them off on the door so they will hang straight together and one side does not become higher or wider than the other. Follow the guidelines for making a standard wreath.

WREATH OF BRANCHES

This contemporary-looking wreath made entirely of tree branches must be made while the branches are still pliable—during the summer. Gather the branches during the early summer and remove all the leaves. Bend the boughs around in a circle, working them together as you go, letting all the secondary twigs find their own place. Add layer upon layer, wiring as you add new branches. When the wreath is full, twist the end of the wire around one of the branches to hold it in place securely. Paint the wreath white. Let it dry and paint it again and again until it is completely covered.

Because this must be constructed a long time before Christmas, when the trees are in leaf, there is plenty of time to test different trims before the season arrives. When the holiday begins, presto! you are ready.

LIVING TOPIARIES

Begin by constructing a hollow topiary form, or purchase one. If it is not already filled, stuff the smallest, outside parts first (arms, ears, tails) packing damp sphagnum moss into the form as tightly as you can. Stuff the main body part last.

Distribute the plants evenly over the body, inserting them into the body of the animal by creating little holes or pockets for the roots with a pointed object. I often find I can separate some of the plants into several portions, taking care that each part has roots. Cover the form with sheet moss surrounding but not burying each plant, using fishing line wrapped about the form to hold it in place. When you finish wrapping the moss with the clear line, tie the end of the line tightly onto a fern pin and push the pin into the packed moss. Fishing line often works loose, so be sure to make several knots and dab them with a little glue to make certain they will hold. Try to finish wrapping so the line ends underneath the form and no mechanics are visible.

To make the topiary more attractive before it is fully covered by the plant material, carefully mix yellow and green food coloring in a spray bottle containing some water. You will have to experiment with the color on a separate piece of moss to achieve the best shade. Try to approximate the color of living moss — not too blue a green.

Depending upon the form you use, you may need to buy eyes and noses in a craft store. As a substitute, buttons without button-holes work well. Trim your topiary for Christmas with fresh holly and a bright bow.

If you wish to use your topiary as a centerpiece, instead of covering it with green sheet moss, cover the surface completely with fresh flowers. Long-lasting flowers such as chrysanthemums seem to work well. Cut the stems very short, about 1/2". Pass a piece of wire through the head of the flower and down the stem, if possible. Push the wired stem into the wet moss. The short stem and the underside of the flower will take up enough moisture to keep it fresh. If you are making this decoration a day ahead, refrigerate it until showtime. This is not a long-lasting decoration, but it is effective. Remember to place the topiary on a plate or tray because it is wet. The number of flowers you will need depends entirely on the size of the form you are using and how much coverage of flowers is needed. The size of the flower heads also depends upon the size of the form. Larger frames need more and larger flowers. Chrysanthemum flowers can be scaled down in size by removing their outer petals one by one until the size is right. This works only with very fresh flowers; older flowers will shatter completely when the petals are removed.

Keep a living topiary damp at all times, and provide enough light for the plants to grow. Remember that the roots are planted fairly deeply inside the moss, so don't let them die from lack of water. Misting during the winter months helps to supply the necessary humidity.

Should your plants all die for one reason or another, let the form dry out completely. Then turn it into an artificial topiary by using small pieces of artificial plants to cover the surface, pinning them in place with filly fern pins which have been touched with hot glue. As long as it is not placed in a bright light, the artificial leaves will not be too noticeable and it will still provide a pleasant decoration.

GARLANDS AND SWAGS

Garlands are not difficult to make, but they are time-consuming. Certain garlands can be made from materials that do not require water, and others can be made in advance and kept fresh by being refrigerated or laid outside on the cold ground out of the sunshine. My friend Ellie keeps hers under a broadleaf evergreen tree in case of snow. As long as the weather is not so bitterly cold that the garlands will freeze, there is usually enough moisture in the ground to keep the greens alive. If the weather is very dry, garlands must be misted periodically to keep them fresh.

To make a fresh garland from evergreens such as Fraser fir, pine, and cedar, wire short lengths of greens together with a continuous roll of fine wire. Keep the pieces short, about 6" long, to allow the garland to be more graceful. If the pieces are too long, garland elbows will jut out at odd angles, defeating the purpose of creating graceful curves.

Another way of making a garland is the rope method. I like to use 1/2" thick jute, which is brown. Using a roll of wire, attach lengths of greenery to the rope, covering the jute completely. This makes a very thick garland and provides a base from which to work other materials into the greens. Small tubes of water can even be wired into the greens so that fresh flowers may be introduced into the garland. Berries, pinecones, and Christmas ornaments can be attached easily onto this type of roping. This is a very time-consuming project, but well worth the effort if you are having a special holiday celebration.

Another kind of fresh garland is made by using long strips from a roll of chicken wire bent around to form tubes that are joined together along the open edge with wire. Before joining the edges together, when the chicken wire is still flat, pack the center with damp sphagnum moss. Then lace the tubing together. Cover the chicken wire by inserting fresh greens through the wire into the damp moss. The moss should be fully packed to give good stability when the greens are inserted. Baby's breath, fresh flowers, wired pinecones and ornaments, whatever your imagination dictates can be pushed into the damp moss. Completely covering the wire is essential. This type of garland is magnificent, much thicker than any of the others.

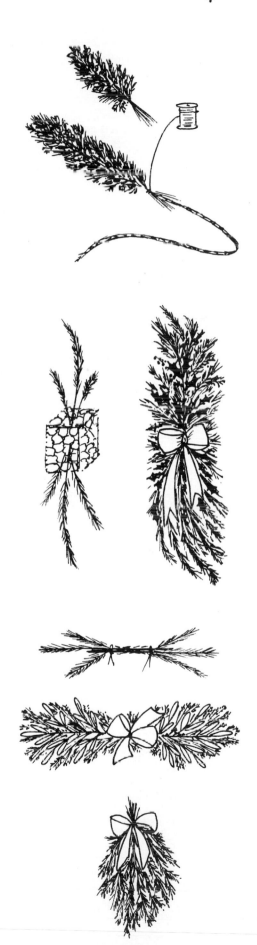

If you are interested in making an artificial garland, use the finest materials you can find because it will last for years. Using the rope method, work vines of artificial greens closely together onto a rope just as you would with live greens until the rope is completely covered. Adding a few pinecones at spots along the garland will help relieve some of the artificial look. Small pieces of Spanish moss can be hot-glued into any bare spots left on the rope. This will also enliven the artificial materials.

Sweet gum balls make an interesting garland. Using an electric drill with a very small bit, drill a hole through each gum ball. String the gum balls on a long, fine wire or strong black thread. If you make the garland long enough, you can double it, twisting the lengths together to create a multi strand wreath that will be flexible. Simply wire the ends together at the top, add a bow, and hang it. I paint sweet gum balls with glossy wood tone paint or liquid brown shoe polish to give them a uniform color.

Real and artificial garlands purchased from the store are big time-savers. In an artificial garland of fine quality, each sprig of artificial green has a wire stem, making it easy to bend it into position. I like to use fresh holly sprigs intermingled in an artificial garland. Usually the holly stems can be pushed under the wired leaves on the garland and no further mechanics are necessary. At the end of the holiday, the dried materials can be removed and the garland carefully packed away for another year.

For less motivated decorators, buying store-made garlands of evergreens and doubling them to make them fuller is a quick and easy substitute for making your own. Any sort of decoration can be wired into place on the doubled garland.

A **swag** is an attractive alternative to a wreath for Christmas. It is simpler to make and uses much less material. An assortment of evergreens can be used.

For mechanics use a cage or make your own of chicken wire wrapped around floral foam. The finished swag should be either a graceful curling design or a sharply-defined placque. Estimate the finished size of the swag and cut the first branch one-half of that length. Do the same for the bottom of the swag. Insert these two pieces into the wet foam. Add shorter helper pieces on both sides of the first branches. Finally fill out the swag using short pieces of greens to give depth and a central focus to the design. At this point add any cones, berries, or other trims by wiring them into place. Cover the cage completely with little bits of greenery. Add a bow and hang!

A simpler swag can be created by gathering several green boughs together and attaching them with wire. Select two pieces for the top and bottom, placing them beside each other going in the opposite direction and overlapping in the center. Wire them together securely because they are the base for everything that is added. Add decreasingly smaller pieces and wire each piece in place as it is positioned. The stems should continue to overlap in the center. When it is full enough, wire trims to the center and add a large bow to camouflage raw ends.

An even simpler swag can be constructed by gathering a few pieces of evergreens together, wiring them together with all the boughs hanging down, and trying a ribbon at the top.

The last two swags can be used outside on the ground in a cemetery, on top of an empty window box, or on a wall or door.

DESIGN FOR THE CORNER OF A DOOR

Cage of wet floral foam
Nails or hook by which design can
  be hung
Strong wire
Staple gun

Wire clippers
Greens — holly, pine, boxwood,
  magnolia, etc.
Trims — pinecones, berries, etc.
Ribbon and ornaments

There are doors that do not lend themselves to decoration. If you have a particularly beautiful front door of magnificent panelled wood, or a heavy glass door, a design placed over one side of the door frame would be most appropriate.

Attach a cage filled with wet floral foam securely to the corner of the frame. It is much easier to work this design in position than to work it elsewhere and move it.

Start in the middle of the cage and create a center of interest. Magnolia leaves and holly are effective. Since magnolia branches are usually thick and awkward to use, I wire individual leaves to floral picks for ease in handling. Berried branches, pinecones on picks, or other ornaments can be added. Boxwood is a good filler for covering the cage.

Next build the design across the top of the door and down the side by choosing two long branches of greens, one for the top and one for the side, and insert them through the cage into the foam. The side piece should be longer than the one for the top. Inserting branches into the foam will cause the release of water from the foam, so be prepared to mop. To hold the design in place, attach these two branches to the framework of the doorway in several places with a staple gun. Insert additional shorter pieces of greens into the foam in each direction, following the lines of the primary pieces.

If additional greens are needed to fill in holes, they may be wired to the primary branches. Because the visual weight in this design is in the focal point, the branches extending across the top and down the side do not have to be full. Add a puffy bow with long streamers that can later be woven into the greenery. If you do not care to use a bow, cluster some beautiful ribbon-trimmed Christmas balls for the center.

If your door swings into the house, any overhanging material will not be affected; however, if the door opens to the outside, be sure all excess material is clipped away from the door's path or your whole design may come tumbling down. Scale is most important in this design. More visual weight should be coming down the side of the door than going across the top of the frame.

An urn or cache pot of greens placed on the opposite side of the entranceway from the corner design will balance the appearance of the doorway.

WINDOW BOX TREATMENT

There is nothing prettier than a window box overflowing with beautiful flowers all summer long, but how disappointing to see it during winter when it becomes bedraggled! This can be remedied without much expense or effort. If your property has any evergreens, they can be pressed into service. If not, a trip to the local garden center or Christmas supply store will produce the small amount of greenery needed.

Prepare the box by removing any dead material which remains. Then dig a little trench along the length of the box, leaving soil still packed along both sides. Fill the trench with blocks of wet floral foam, end to end. Pack the soil around the foam to make it steady in the box.

Fill the box with cut pieces of evergreen 8" to 10" in length inserted into the wet foam. Use a variety of greens to give color and textural interest. The greens will remain fresh for a long time because the foam will collect any rain or snow that may fall. Even if the weather becomes freezing, the greens will be supplied with water on days when there is some thawing. If you live where the weather remains warm, the box can be watered just as if it were full of fresh plants.

Another window box treatment is one that I have used for many years. I place the row of greens in the back half of the box next to the window, and in front of the greens sprinkle bird seed on top of the soil. The birds love it, and provide daily activity which is delightful to see from inside. Because the evergreens shield observers from the birds' view, it is possible to sit right next to the window and watch. This is especially entertaining for someone who is house-bound.

Window boxes can be trimmed with all manner of materials, including artificial greens, but do not use material inappropriate to the season of the year or the geographical location of the box.

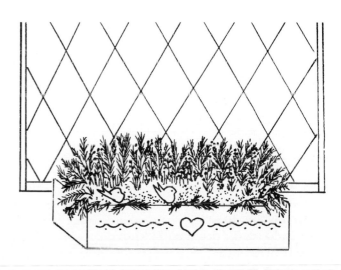

Wired Cone

Split Cones

Suggestions for materials for a
pod and cone wreath

White pine cones
Sugar pine cones
Hemlock cones
Spruce cones
Larch cones
Scotch pine cones
Fir cones
Sweet gum balls
Iris pods
Okra pods
Peach stones, dried and cleaned
Chestnut burrs
Acorns
Hickory nuts
Walnuts in their shells
Pecans in shells
Lotus pods
Strelitzia pods
Magnolia pods
Brazil nuts
Deer moss
Dried pepper berries
Dried whole spices
Avocado seeds, dried and cleaned
Eucalyptus buds

PINECONE AND POD WREATH

A piece of 1/4" plywood, at least 18" square
Electric or hand-held jig saw
Sand paper
Electric drill and drill bit
Assortment of pods, nuts, and cones
Spool of #24 wire
Hot glue gun
White craft glue
Evergreens, boxwood, or magnolia leaves
Brown felt

There are several ways to construct a pinecone and pod wreath. If you have the time—and it will take quite a bit—and the patience, wreaths of wired cones and pods are the best. A wooden wreath form will be necessary for all of them.

Take the piece of plywood or masonite and find the center by drawing two diagonal lines to connect opposite corners of the board. Draw a circle with the diameter you want for your wreath around the center point—16" is a good size. Make another circle 3" inside the first circle. Cut around both circles to make the wreath form. Sand the rough edges. With an electric drill, make holes evenly over the surface of the form—about 3/4" apart. Using the wreath form as a pattern, cut a piece of brown felt in the same size and shape.

Lay out cones for the outside edge of the wreath, making them all approximately the same size and variety. I like to use long, slender cones because I like the appearance of the tapered ends. White pine is good for this. Make certain there are enough cones to complete the circle. It is aggravating to run short of material when you are not quite finished.

Place the middle of an 8" length of wire around the bottom row of scales of each cone and twist the wire tightly so it is fixed firmly to the cone. Repeat on the other side so every cone will have two wires coming from each side. All the cones in the wreath should be wired in this way.

Attach a cone to the wreath ring by inserting the wires from each side of the cone into different holes and then twisting them together underneath. Each cone should be firmly set in place. If it is not, untwist the wires and pull them tighter so the cone moves as little as possible. Clip off extra wire.

Work the outside edge first, then the inner edge, and finally the center. Try to form a pattern with the materials for the viewer's eye to follow. Everything should seem to be moving in the same direction. To add interest, some of the cones could be cut crosswise to form attractive slices that have the appearance of rosettes. Do not use materials with torn or scruffy edges.

When all the wiring is done, there may be a few holes to fill. Use a hot glue gun to dab a little glue onto the back of small pods or cones to fill these places.

A wire for hanging can be worked into the outside rim of the wreath by attaching it to some of the wires which have been used to secure the cones in place, or you can staple a wire hanger onto the back of the completed wreath. Do not allow the wire to extend beyond the edges of the wreath.

Finally, give the whole wreath a coating of lacquer or glossy wood-tone paint to add luster to the pods and cones, as well as added protec-

tion. When the wreath is dry, glue the piece of brown felt over the unfinished side.

When you hang the wreath, you may wish to add greenery. I have used sprigs of polished boxwood inserted between cones. The boxwood lasts quite a long time. Fraser fir is another good choice of filler since its needles do not drop readily. Polished magnolia leaves make a lustrous backing. If the wreath is to rest on a table, the magnolia leaves will slide underneath easily. For a hanging wreath, they should be stapled to the underside. Make sure the stems do not show.

It is possible to hot-glue all of the material to the wreath form, but a wreath made this way will not be as substantial. If linoleum paste is used instead of hot glue, the cones may continue to be re-positioned as long as the adhesive is still soft—good to know if you are not pleased with the design.

An old pinecone wreath can be given new life with a coat of white or gold paint.

STAIRWAYS

No matter what the architectural design of a staircase, it provides an ideal setting for decorations. Often there is a newel post supporting the banister at the end of the stairs. This can be decorated with swags, garlands, or a bouquet of flowers with streamers cascading the length of the post.

The stairs themselves usually have a small ledge outside the balustrades where greens can be placed. If your stairway is divided by a landing, this area can become an additional focal point for a prominent decoration —a large wreath, swag, or even a Christmas tree if you have the space. Often a graceful curving staircase will have space underneath the stairs which can be filled with a profusion of flowering plants for Christmas. There are almost always spaces between the balustrades where ornaments can be suspended on bright ribbons.

Be sure to fasten any decoration securely to its location, and make certain nothing interferes with movement on the steps. The handrail must be free for use, so suspend garlands under the banister, if possible, or provide space for the hand to grip every few inches. Wires, staples and strong floral adhesive tape make it easy to attach any design anywhere you wish to place it.

Don't forget the outside entrance stairs. Pots of greens or softly glowing luminaries can welcome guests. Tall garden torches, used often in the summer, can be used at Christmas as well. If they are tall, they can be trimmed with greens and ribbons streaming down like Christmas banners. In the winter, if the ground is so hard that nothing can be inserted, they can be mounted in clay pots.

To do this, use a pot large enough to balance the size of the torch you are using. Use another pot, preferably plastic, inside the clay pot as a liner. Wrap the end of the torch in aluminum foil. Mix plaster of Paris according to the directions on the package and pour it into the liner. Insert the wrapped torch into the plaster and let it stay until the plaster scts up. Remove the torch. The foil will stay in place in the plaster making a permanent hole in which to place the torch whenever you wish to use it in a pot. The outer pot is not damaged and can be used for other purposes. When you want to use the torch, just place the liner back in the pot and insert the torch once more. Fill the top of the liner with greens, moss, or mulch.

BOXWOOD KISSING BALL

Two Iglu Grande holders wired
   together
      or
Floral foam bound with floral adhesive tape
      or
Floral foam wrapped in chicken
   wire

Popsicle stick or wooden tongue
   depressor
Wire to make a hanger
Half-bushel of boxwood sprigs
   about 5" long
Wooden floral picks with wire
Ribbon
Plant polish, optional
Trims and holly, optional

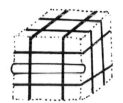

Although there are many ways to make a kissing ball, this is the one I use. I find it more satisfactory than using a potato or grapefruit which I have also tried. The wet foam can be kept moist by watering the entire ornament occasionally over a sink so the boxwood stays fresher.

If you are not using Oasis Iglu Grande cages, wrap a 4" square chunk of dry Oasis in a grid of green floral tape, overlapping the ends of the tape so they adhere to each other and not the foam. While wrapping with the tape, place a wooden popsicle stick or tongue depressor across the bottom of the piece of foam, wrapping the tape over it as you work. The stick will provide a firm support for the hanging wire. Or, you could cover your chunk of foam with chicken wire fastened securely all around.

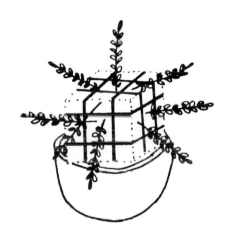

Soak the boxwood overnight in warm water before using it, and submerge the floral foam in water until it stops bubbling. Insert a long wire, which will be used for hanging, down through the foam, over the stick or cage and back up through the foam again. Secure the wire by twisting the ends together, and make a loop where the hanging ribbon will be attached. Tie on a bit of ribbon so you can find the loop when the kissing ball is filled in. Now you are ready to begin making the ball.

The pieces of boxwood should all be about 4" to 5" long. Insert a piece in the top of the ball, then the bottom, then one on each side to form a skeleton framework. All the pieces must be about the same length so the ball will be round and even. If the finished ball looks a little ragged, it can always be trimmed. Be sure to cover all the foam and mechanics.

As you work on the kissing ball, you must keep turning it so it will not lose its roundness. I use a small bowl as a holder as I work so the leaves will not be crushed. This is much easier than trying to work on it while it is hanging and swinging in the air. After the kissing ball has been completed, I give it a quick spritz with plant polish. This gives the leaves a pleasing lustrous shine.

Make sure the wire loop is hidden by boxwood when attaching the ribbon hanger at the top. The bottom bow, or streamers, can be added by wiring them onto a wooden pick and inserting the pick into the foam. Otherwise the bow will fall out.

Trimming a kissing ball is a matter of choice. A few sprigs of polished holly with berries may be enough. Another time you may wish to insert small bunches of herbs which have been wired to a pick. Garlands of tiny beads could trim a very formal kissing ball if the garlands are draped into swags and secured with fern pins into the foam. For a party, fresh flowers could be inserted into the foam.

MY FAVORITE TREE

1/2" plywood triangle, 17" base with 20" sides	Staple gun
Dark green paint	Boxwood, pine, holly
Wet floral foam	Pump-spray bottle of leaf polish
Chicken wire	Real bird's nest, if you can find one
Piece of tree bark, 3" wide by 5" high	Artificial birds
	Wire
	Popcorn and cranberries

I first made this door decoration many years ago and it is still one of the most popular decorations I make. I have made them for sale and for my own home; variations of the design have won blue ribbons in several Christmas flower shows. No wonder it is my favorite tree!

It is best to make this tree over the kitchen sink since quantities of water will escape from the wet foam as the greens are inserted. I usually let the tree drain overnight before placing it in its spot on the door or wall. Since making this decoration is very time consuming, do it several days ahead of the time you want to use it. As long as the foam is kept moist it will last long time.

Cut a triangular piece of 1/2" plywood, 20" by 20" by 17", and paint it dark green. Try to find a piece of natural tree bark, 3" by 5". It may be necessary to find a larger piece and split it so it will lie flat. Nail it to the bottom center of the triangle to create a tree trunk for the design.

Place chunks of soaked floral foam on top of the wooden triangle and cover the entire frame with chicken wire which is then stapled into place along the edge of the triangle. This creates a strong cage to hold the wet foam. The foam does not need to come all the way to the edge of the triangle.

To create the tree itself, push boxwood pieces about three to four inches long into the wet foam. Begin with the outside edges, extending each piece beyond the edge of the frame following the tree shape. Fill in the center of the tree last using shorter pieces of boxwood, still placing the boxwood to give the effect of tree branches. Cover the chicken wire completely.

Add a few pieces of holly and white pine at random, clipping the pine to make it look fuller. Spray the tree with leaf polish so the leaves will have a soft shine.

Trim the tree with an abandoned bird's nest, if you can find one. Wire it into place near the bottom of the tree just above the trunk. Make a large U-shaped wire pin and push it through the nest and into the foam, slanting the pin downward so the nest cannot pull out. Put an artificial sitting bird into the nest and fix it firmly into place with a wire. If you are unable to find a true bird's nest, create one by using a handful of Spanish moss molded into nest shape and reinforced with a few twigs.

Scatter a few more pretty birds throughout the tree. Garlands of white popcorn and cranberries can be added. Be careful that the garlands do not overpower the birds. Add a small bow under the bird's nest for an extra burst of color.

There are two ways to hang this tree. Either drill two holes straight through the plywood in the center about three-fourths of the way up and

Clipped White Pine

drive two sturdy nails through the holes and into the door, or staple a strong piece of wire to the top of the tree to form a hanger. This must be firmly stapled into the wood because the piece will be heavy when complete. I have found it hangs best from the top of the door instead of on the front of the door when a wire hanger is used.

There are many variations on this design. If you do not want to use birds, fresh flowers, tiny tree ornaments, or bows can be used. Another variation is to make the plywood background in another shape—a star, a bell, an angel. Just be certain, if your tree is going outside, to select weather-resistant decorations. Inside, just about anything goes.

When the holidays are over, the boxwood and Oasis can be pulled out of the frame, and the frame and decorations saved for another year.

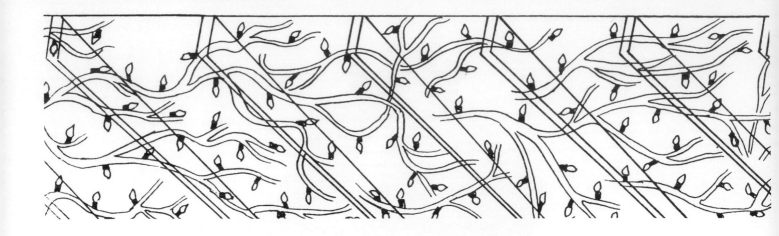

BEAMED CEILING TREATMENT

Several years ago a young friend of mine, Toby Hoblitzell, decorated his family's dining room for Christmas. They had a wonderful beamed ceiling which was the perfect spot for Toby's creativity. He selected many small tree branches and painted them all white. After the paint had dried, he proceeded to attach them to the beams by wiring them to small screw eyes inserted directly into the beams.

He then wound strings of tiny white lights, with a white cord, around the branches. The light strands plugged into each other so there was only one continuous strand travelling throughout the ceiling, ending with a single plug inconspicuously entering a receptacle. The branches made a fascinating pattern on the ceiling, and when the lights were turned on, it was magnificent!

Christmas ornaments, with their pinpoints of reflected lights echoing the gleam of the tiny white lights, were hung at intervals adding a touch of magic. Quite an ambitious undertaking, but well worth the effort.

A less involved ceiling treatment can be accomplished with garlands of greens entwined with fanciful ribbons. Again, screw eyes should be inserted into the beams and the garlands attached by wires to the screw eyes. A staple gun might be used if screw eyes are not available. If the beams are painted, then repairs can easily be made when the decoration is dismantled. Staples leave a tiny hole which can be filled with white toothpaste or spackle after the staple removal, and then touched with paint.

Christmas ornaments can be attached to the garlands after they are in position to add a little glitz. There are glittered sticks available that can be intermingled with the greens to add sparkle without the use of lights.

Garlands of flowers can be created by using fine quality silk flowers attached to roping. The roping could be artificial or fresh-cut, or it could even be the beautiful silk braid roping which is sold for drapery work. The flowers should have their stems removed as is done in fresh flower leis, and they should be strung together in one continuous vine. Wire or wrap the lei of flowers around the garland. Select flowers for this project by determining the maximum overall size of your room, using small flowers for a small room and larger flowers for a more impressive setting.

A less pretentious treatment for ceiling beams is to drape ribbons throughout the ceiling, accented by bunches of dried flowers. Test different positions for the nosegays before securing them into place, always view them from below to achieve the proper perspective.

APPLE FAN

1/2" plywood cut into a semi-circle
Green paint
Brightly polished red apples
Pineapple, medium size, if desired
Sprigs of washed boxwood and
  holly
Polished magnolia leaves
Pinecones, optional
Staple gun
Hammer
Drill with small bit

Roll of #26 wire for pinecones, if
  used
#8 finishing nails, one for each
  apple
Three #10 nails for a pineapple
Triangle of wood 1" thick, 17" high,
  5 1/2" base
  or
Two steel braces with screws, if
  design is to stand

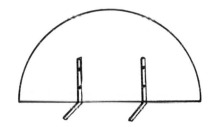

Cut the plywood in a semi-circle to fit the space where the completed fan will be used. My fireplace fan is 36" wide by 18" high. Attach a supporting triangle of wood or metal braces if it will be used free-standing. Paint the wood dark green.

Arrange magnolia leaves, slightly overlapping, around the outside edges of the board. On the bottom edge the leaves should lie sideways. Staple them in place. Arrange a second row of magnolia leaves overlapping the first row and staple them in place. Lay the pineapple in the center of the fan, and place the apples in position around the pineapple. All the apples should be facing in the same direction.

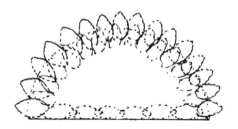

Carefully remove the pineapple, and hammer 3 nails into the center of the fan to hold the pineapple in place. Nails should be set at an upward-tilting angle to prevent the pineapple from falling. Push the pineapple onto the nails.

Remove the apples, one by one, and drive a finishing nail into place for each. These nails should also be angled slightly upward to hold the apples securely. Impale each apple on its respective nail. If you wish to use pinecones in the design, place them in position, then drill a hole on both sides of each cone so wires inserted through the plywood can hold them in place. Tuck fresh boxwood and holly in any open spaces.

To use the fan above an outside door, one with an ornate decorated molding above the door frame, support the fan on a ridge of the frame and, using two nails, attach the fan to the molding. You can tell by looking at your own door whether or not a fan will fit over it. If you are using this design on an inside wall, a heavy nail must be used in two places to secure the design to the wall. It could be used on a mantelpiece if the mantel is wide enough to carry it. Braces should have been added to the back of a fan made for the fireplace before decorating.

An apple fan can also be made using artificial magnolia leaves and artificial apples on 1/4" plywood. Fresh greens should be added to give some life to the design. This will be much lighter in weight. I have never seen an artificial pineapple which really resembles a fresh one, so omit it altogether if you decide to make the artificial version. It can be just as effective with a Santa or a focal point made of pinecones. An artificial apple fan, except for the fresh material, need not be taken apart. Store it in a plastic bag and bring it out again next year, refreshed with new evergreens.

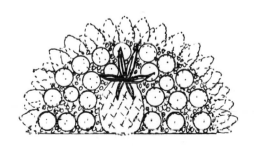

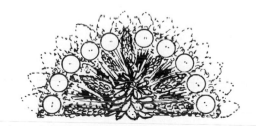

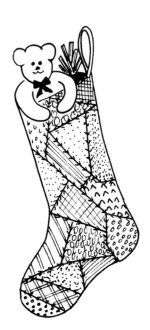

Mistletoe

FIREPLACES, MANTELS, AND HEARTHS

The fireplace is a gathering spot, especially at Christmas, and often becomes the focal point of family activities.

Mantelpieces offer a stage of sorts on which to display prized collectibles trimmed with a few greens. Arrangements of any kind for the mantel can be either symmetrical or asymmetrical. A center design establishes a symmetrical setting, which should be evenly flanked by candle-sticks or other accents. Asymmetrical placement of disparate articles dictates the need to balance the visual weight of the decorative objects on either side of the mantel. Arrangements of fresh materials for a mantelpiece can cover the entire length of the mantel or only portions of it. A central design should cover about one third of the space on the mantel. An arrangement which is part of an asymmetrical design should occupy about one fourth of the length of the mantel, balanced carefully with objects on the other end.

When arranging flowers for a mantelpiece, try to do the arrangement in place. Usually the height of the mantel is just above eye level, so doing the greens and flowers "on location" can be beneficial for positioning the material. Some of the flowers should face down towards the viewer. Others should face upward and to the side. If you do the arrangement elsewhere and move it to the mantel, you may find yourself looking at the underside of the flowers. Have some of the material reach over the edge of the mantel, sweeping gracefully down, to give a full and opulent look. This not only applies to flowers, but to arrangements of Christmas greens and ornaments as well. If necessary, lengthen the wires on ornaments by adding a doubled #18 wire taped to the original ornament stem. This will make the new stem strong enough to enable you to place it into a downward-facing position without fear that it will come loose from the base mechanics.

Small Christmas trees can be used as a focal point in the center of a mantel or they can be grouped to one side. Candles are important accessories whether they are used flanking a central design, grouped at one end, or used throughout the entire length of the mantel. Small flower arrangements can be anchored above or below the mantelpiece. Oasis Iglus, attached to the wood through their side tabs, are good to use for this.

The hearth is a prominent display area especially if it is raised. Polished brass containers can be filled with greens and Christmas ornaments, or a wooden basket of fatwood kindling can be trimmed with bright ribbons. Flowering Christmas plants are effective banked together near a hearth.

Garlands can be used above or below the mantel, but care must be taken not to have them too near the fire. Artificial flame-retardant garlands are appropriate in this area.

Above the mantel your usual mirror or painting could be replaced with a wreath at Christmas using tiny white lights on a battery pack to brighten the scene in the evening. If you leave the mirror or painting in place, then trim it with a garland of greens and ribbons to catch the eye. Although important works of art need no accessorizing, often at Christmas a spray of magnolia leaves placed behind the painting can impart a

sense of festivity.

A handmade Christmas stocking to hang from the mantel often becomes a cherished heirloom. Needlepoint has come a long way since I attempted my first piece as a young girl. Today's needlepoint is dazzling and sophisticated. My friend Barbara Budlow owns a delightful store in the Village of Cross Keys in Baltimore called "Fancy Work," where there is such an assortment of Christmas items to stitch that it is difficult to choose just one. They can be worked in a variety stitches and they are embellished with sequins, beads, bugles, and pearls! The most important thing to remember about Christmas needlepoint is that it takes a long time to have your work blocked and backed so there is always a cut-off date for getting projects completed in time for Christmas. And that date is long before the actual holiday!

BOXWOOD TOPIARY TREE

Planter with liner	Green floral adhesive tape
Plaster of Paris	Wire
Tree branch or painted dowel	Spahgnum moss or sheet moss
Cage of wet floral foam	Additional evergreen sprigs for trim,
Boxwood	if desired
Ribbons and trims	Vine to decorate trunk, if desired

Topiaries take time to construct so begin at at least a day or so in advance of the time you wish to use them. Store them in an extra refrigerator or outside under cover if it is cold. Because they are made with wet floral foam, water can be added every few days to keep the boxwood fresh. I have had them last a month if they have been kept cool and damp.

Select a planter—ceramic cache pot, brass planter, or clay pot—and line it with a plastic insert. The liner is necessary to hold the plaster of Paris. A clay pot will be cracked by plaster as it expands and dries if no liner is used. Also, if a liner is used, it is possible to remove the liner holding the plaster and the trunk, saving it for use another time, and have the use of the planter for another purpose. If you are using a small container, you can use a strong plastic bag as a liner.

Determine the size of your completed tree and cut the tree trunk accordingly. Cut the bottom of the trunk straight so it can rest firmly against the bottom of the planter and cut the other end to a point so it can be inserted into the cage holding the foam. A curving branch may be chosen for the trunk, but for the topiary itself to be straight the center of the ball of greens must be directly over the pot.

Mix plaster of Paris according to the directions on the box and pour immediately into the liner which has already been placed inside the planter. Immediately put the prepared tree trunk into the wet plaster and hold it steady for a few minutes until the plaster sets up. Let the plaster harden for a few hours.

Begin the next stage by attaching a cage filled with wet floral foam to the top of the trunk. When this is secure, place three small nails around the trunk just under the cage, or make a ridge of wire wrapped with green floral adhesive tape. Either of these devices will be a barrier to keep the cage from slipping down the trunk.

At this point if you wish to decorate the trunk with a pretty vine, attach the top of the vine to the trunk with a staple just under the barrier below the cage. Wrap the vine down and around the trunk gracefully and staple the lower end to the trunk inside the planter above the plaster. The vine should appear to be growing around the tree trunk from inside the container.

Decide what size the finished ball of plant material should be and cut the lengths of boxwood accordingly. Insert stems of boxwood into the top, bottom, and around the sides to establish the size of the completed design. If the design seems too small or too large, it can be corrected at this point. Fill in all the way around. Make it full and round and be sure no mechanics are showing.

The topiary may be sheared to make a smooth ball or only lightly pruned. This is a personal choice. However if small ornaments or garlands are to be added as trims, they may disappear into foliage that has not been trimmed.

Topiaries may be trimmed or left undecorated. Before trimming, cover the top of the plaster by mounding with damp moss or wood chips. The choice really depends upon the planter and how it will look best. Just be sure to pile up enough material at the base of the trunk so that it does not look flat.

To trim a topiary with fruit, the construction changes slightly. When the skeleton of greens is satisfactory, attach the fruit to the lower half of the topiary. For each piece of fruit, take a long sturdy wire and bend it into a U. Push the wire through the fruit from the bottom, and insert the wired fruit into the cage holding the foam. Then green-in around the fruit so the greens can help support the fruit. The fruits used on the top half of the design can be positioned by fixing them on straight wires and inserting them directly into the foam after the greens are in place. When wiring fruit for the top of a topiary, wrap the wire with green floral tape so the fruit does not slip down the wire. I use two or three #18 wires wrapped together with tape for this procedure.

Almost any trim used on a topiary will have to be wired in place. Even ornaments that come with an attached wire will need to have their wires strengthened and lengthened for most topiaries. Ribbons and streamers should be applied last. Streamers falling from beneath the topiary can be made by gathering several folded lengths of ribbon together in the center using a long U-shaped wire. Twist the wire to hold the ribbon and then push the wire through the greens right into the mechanics. The length of each streamer should be slightly different to carry the eye down the trunk to the base.

If, instead of a vine, you are going to wind a ribbon around the trunk, staple or glue it under the cage at the top, and at the bottom fix it in place above the edge of the damp moss so it will not absorb any moisture.

Another way to decorate the planter is to repeat the use of fresh-cut boxwood around the base. To do this, soak pieces of floral foam and put them into strong plastic bags with their tops rolled down. The bags will become liners. Pieces of boxwood can be inserted into the foam to create an effect that is full and lush.

Fresh flowers are beautiful in a topiary when they are placed into vials of water that can then be inserted into the tree. However, unless it is a very long water vial, a wire will have to be attached with floral tape so the flower holder can be firmly fixed in place. Occasionally you may eliminate the tube of water and insert the flower stem directly into the wet foam.

Garlands of beads can be draped around the topiary if they are secured to the design at intervals with a U-shaped wire. This gives a beautiful effect on closely cropped boxwood.

If the topiary itself is to have no decorations, heap small fruits and clusters of grapes over the mound of moss at the base.

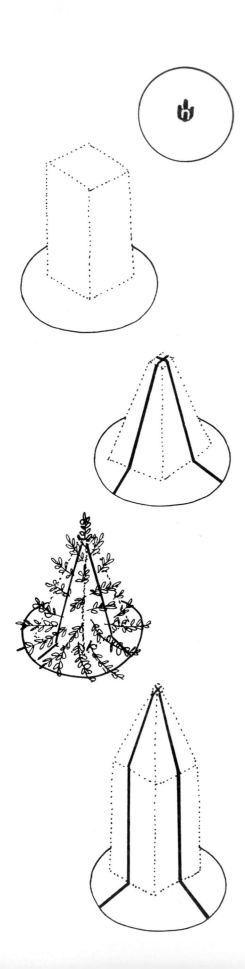

BOXWOOD CHRISTMAS TREE

Freshly-cut boxwood, a paper
  market bag full
1 block of wet floral foam
Green floral adhesive tape

Floral clay
Floral foam spike
Clear plate, 10" diameter
Ribbons, trims

Soak the boxwood in water overnight. This cleans the leaves and the material will stay fresh longer.

Anchor a floral foam spike to a plate with floral adhesive. Stand a brick of wet floral foam upright on the spike. Shape the foam by slicing off the top edges with a knife so it resembles a pyramid. Leave an uncut square on the top of the block. Run a long, narrow piece of green floral adhesive tape up, over, and down the foam, fixing the tape to itself underneath the plate. Be sure the plate is dry so the adhesive will stick. Do this in both directions so the tree will not topple. Using the spike alone is not satisfactory because of the weight of the finished tree.

Establish the height of the tree with a piece of boxwood inserted into the top. Then establish the width of the tree by inserting pieces of boxwood around the bottom and at various levels up the sides of the foam. Keep the tree shape in mind while doing this. It should be narrower at the top. Now you have a skeleton to work within. Proceed to green-in the entire tree so no foam or tape is visible. The boxwood should cover the plate and extend over it for an inch or two. The tree should be full and fat when complete, but it should still have the shape of a tree.

Decorating the tree is a matter of choice. If you like a natural look, insert some holly and a few pieces of cut white pine into the boxwood. When using white pine, cut off the tips of the needles. This eliminates any dry brown edges and makes the pine look fuller. A dusting of plant polish over the entire tree will give it a soft shine. Additional materials such as berries, bows, garlands, and ornaments must be attached to wires long enough to be inserted through the boxwood and into the foam. Select something appropriate for the top of the tree; such as an angel, Santa, or star, which must also be put onto a strong wire or pick to reach into the foam.

If additional water is poured into the top of the tree from time to time, it should last throughout the holiday season and beyond.

To make a larger boxwood tree, select a 12" base plate. Attach three foam spikes to the center of the dry plate with clay and stand one brick of wet foam on top of the spikes. Place another half block on top of the first block. For stability, tape two #18 wires together and push them down through the top of the half block into the lower block. Then taper the sides of the top block of foam to suggest a tree form. Tape both blocks into position on the base, wrapping the floral adhesive tape around in both direction and overlapping underneath the base, as in the directions for the smaller tree. The two blocks should not be able to move after they have been taped. Proceed to make a skeleton of boxwood stems around the tree beginning with the top and base circumference. Fill in the tree completely. This tree uses at least another half market bag full of boxwood, but makes a considerably larger tree.

For an even larger tree, make a very sturdy cone of wire, 18" or more high. Turkey wire is better than chicken wire. A cone is made by rolling a quarter circle of chicken or turkey wire into a cone and lacing the edges together with wire. Fill the inside of the cone with either wet sphagnum moss or chunks of wet oasis stuffed into place. Place the cone on a large plastic tray. Lomey makes trays 15" in diameter. Attach a piece of green floral adhesive tape to one of the low wires on the cone and pull the tape over the edge of the base, securing it underneath. Do this in four places around the cone to hold the tree steady on the base. Proceed as for the other trees: first establish the height, fill in around the bottom, make a skeleton framework on the sides, and then fill in the tree completely. No wire should be visible.

The larger trees take a considerable amount of boxwood, but they are very impressive when completed. I use one on my sideboard where I can attach electric tree lights into a receptacle. I do not use battery packs for these large trees since there are not enough lights on the string for my taste. When the holiday season is over, the wire cone can be saved for another year and re-stuffed with fresh material.

A half-tree of boxwood is perfect on a mantelpiece where a full tree would be too large. The front and sides are finished and only the back is not fully filled out. This tree can be used in front of a mirror if it is backed up tightly against it.

Fix a floral spike onto a 5" round plate with floral clay, then press a block of wet floral foam onto it. Trim the top of the foam to a pyramid shape with a small flat top. Fix the foam to the plate with floral adhesive tape, up, over, down and stuck to itself under the plate. If one strip of adhesive is not enough, add a second going in the opposite direction.

Make a skeleton framework by inserting a piece of boxwood for height, several pieces around the bottom, and a few pieces at various points up the sides to establish a symmetrical shape. Do all of this framework on the mantel to get the proper perspective. The boxwood around the bottom should overlap the plate. Turn the tree around and, using very small pieces of boxwood, about 3/4" long, barely cover the wet foam on the back. This is enough to make the tree appear to be finished on all sides. Complete the filling-in.

Try to keep any trims in scale with the size of the tree. Dried flowers tucked among the leaves are soft and pretty. Garlands of fresh cranberries or popcorn add color, and small magnolia or camellia leaves tucked under the bottom edge are a nice finishing touch, but avoid too much overlapping material at the edge of the mantelpiece.

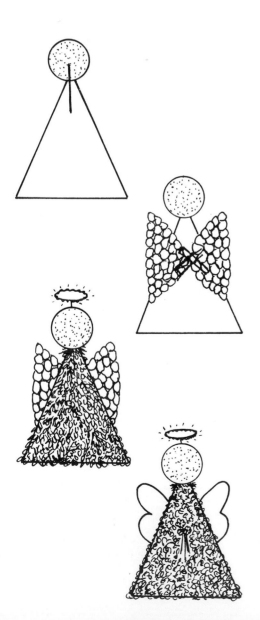

A boxwood angel is really a variation of a boxwood tree with the addition of a head and wings. When the tree is complete, trim the boxwood with clippers so the shape is smooth and slender.

To make the head, take a styrofoam ball and cover small sections of it at a time with hot glue. Roll the glued surface in minced green sheet moss. Craft glue does not have enough body to hold the minced moss, hot glue must be used.

Attach the head to the body by using two #18 straight wires, approximately 12" long, bound together with floral tape. Insert one end into the head and the longer end into the body.

Wings can be made either by cutting them from wire screening and painting them with bright metallic paint, or by bending glittered chenille stems—two for each side—into the outline of wings. Fix the painted screen wings to the body with fern pins—angled to keep the wings from slipping down. For the outlined wings, wire them together and pin them to the back of the angel with a long U-shaped piece of wire.

Make a halo from a piece of glitter wire, leaving a long straight stem to be pushed into the head. If you encounter any problem pushing the glitter wire into the styrofoam, add a piece of #18 wire to the bottom with tape. The wire will go into the styrofoam easily.

I like this angel without arms, hands, or a face, but you can add them if you wish. The wings and halo suggest an angel and I don't think any more is needed. Place the angel in a prominent place surrounded with small votive lights. Add a few fresh flowers in a small bouquet placed on the front where hands might be.

A DESIGN OF FLOWERS
FOR A FAVORITE BOX

Prepare two props to hold the box lid up by using two sticks of the same length or wrap several #18 straight wires with floral tape to do the job. Place a water-tight liner inside the box, any kind will do because it will not be seen, and fill the liner with wet floral foam cut to be higher than the rim of the box. The foam is cut high so material can be inserted at an upward angle to look as if it is flowing downward. Fill with flowers and foliage. To use a box with an un-hinged separate lid, place the top on the table next to the box, using it as an accessory. If the lid is too large, however, it might be best to use it as a base for the box to sit on.

LIGHT FIXTURES

Chandeliers. There are so many different sizes and shapes of chandeliers, it would be difficult to give suggestions for decorating all of them, but here are a few ideas for some of them.

A traditional brass chandelier with four or more arms can easily be draped with an evergreen garland and ribbons. A few ornaments dropping from the lowest parts of the arms can be added. A chain of Christmas tree beads could be intermingled with the garland or the beads could be used alone without any greens. Tissue paper flowers strung closely together make a bright and festive garland, wonderful with a Mexican motif.

A very simple suggestion is to wrap bright ribbon around the arms, tie a bow on each light base, and add a sprig of fresh greens. If children are helping, they could construct small hanging ornaments to be included with the ribbon.

Very small wreaths of fresh or artificial greens can be made to surround each lamp base. Fresh baby's breath is a good choice of material for wreath making. A very small bow can be added for a touch of color.

Crystal chandeliers are so impressive they do not need much embellishment. If there is a center where mechanics can be wired into place, attach a cage or cages of wet floral foam and cover them with galax leaves. Insert stems of white or red euphorbia to spring out in every direction as sprays from a fountain. Euphorbia is a dramatic stem of small flowers and many leaves. Remove all the leaves so only the flowers remain. Seal the ends of the euphorbia by burning them to keep the milky white substance in the stems. You can use them without this treatment, but they will last longer if it is done. In addition to euphorbia, some sprays of white snowflake chrysanthemums—another long-lasting flower—could be added.

Early American fixtures are charming when they are decorated with dried flowers in bunches, or nosegays of fresh baby's breath tied with simple soft ribbon. Bolder ribbons, even prints, could be used. Coarse twine or raffia could be tied into bows to attach a few wooden ornaments. Tin cut-outs could be suspended from ribbon or twine as well. There are many attractive ornaments snipped from tin; but if you cannot find any, use polished or painted cookie cutters as your ornaments. Early American decor does not call for glitter.

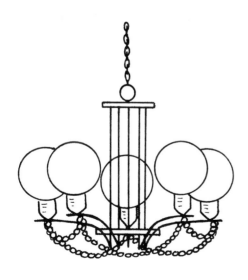

Contemporary light fixtures usually are made from lucite, chrome or polished steel. I have seen a few contemporary brass and chrome chandeliers, but they are the exception. These fixtures have very clean lines with interesting angles to their arms. Often very small bulbs are strung inside lucite tubing. Contemporary design calls for a bold statement without any clutter. To decorate this kind of fixture at Christmas, a single flower in a small tube of water can be tied into place with some spectacular ribbon. Cover the tube of water with the same ribbon before tying it to the fixture. No mechanics should be visible. If a flower does not appeal to you, try a shiny ornament tied with beautiful gold and silver cording. The idea is only to accessorize the fixture, not create clutter.

Any of the chandeliers mentioned can have puffy bows under the center with streamers of ribbons flowing to an object on the table.

Often a chandelier can be enveloped in a cloud of soft chiffon or netting to create an illusion of misty light from within. Flowers, real or artificial, can trim the area where the gathers come together. This look takes a special kind of room as it is quite ornate.

Wall sconces do not require much material to trim them. Chances are there will be some sort of arm which can be used for anchoring decorative materials. If the sconce is metal, cover the arm first with a ribbon that matches the color of the sconce; that is, a silver ribbon for chrome or silver, and gold ribbon for a brass sconce. This prevents scratches when the mechanics are attached.

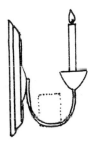

For a single sconce, use a small cage filled with wet floral foam and wire it securely in place. Make sure to cover the floor with newspapers or plastic in the event any water escapes while you are working. Insert greens, berried branches, cones, or ornaments into the foam. Have them cascading out on both sides, or sweeping from one side to the other in a line arrangement. Wait to add ribbon until the design has been completed and the foam has stopped dripping. Water-resistant ribbon can be found for outside wall sconces.

If you are working with a double-arm sconce, it will be more difficult because the center of the fixture has nothing on which to rest the mechanics. This may be remedied by using a dowel, painted dark green, cut long enough to rest across both the arms. Anchor the dowel in place with cord or floral adhesive tape. After one end has been anchored, thread the foam-filled cage onto the dowel, then anchor the other end in place. Christmas greens can then be wired in place to conceal the dowel completely. Proceed to make the arrangement, filling out the cage in whatever design you choose.

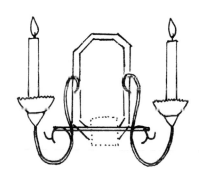

Dried arrangements can be worked the same way, but use an unpainted dowel or paint it to match the design. Instead of Oasis, use Sahara made for silk and dried material.

THE DINING ROOM TABLE

A dining room table provides the perfect setting to exhibit skills in tablescaping—an art form in itself—and Christmas offers almost unlimited possibilities, so bring out the best linens, china, crystal, and your imagination. Entire books have been written on the art of table setting, so I will limit myself to offering a few suggestions that have worked well for me.

There are few restrictions as to what can and cannot be placed in the center of a table in your own home; however, one should be able to see the person on the other side of a dinner table without having to peek through a forest of greenery, and the decorations should not be falling into the place settings. Anything painted for the occasion must have been done days in advance so there will be no lingering odor of paint.

Centerpieces are the focal point of a Christmas table. Make them beautiful with washed and polished greens, shiny fruit, and the freshest flowers. Snowflake chrysanthemums are a favorite of mine at Christmas. They are long-lasting and blend well with almost any evergreen. I often add high-quality silk carnations to my Christmas arrangements. They can be used again and again—an investment in the future.

The placement of the decorative design on the table will determine how the rest of the table is set. Some of the placements I have used over the years are shown. If a table is placed against a wall, or at least not under a chandelier, there is more leeway in the height of the arrangement.

Accenting the tablecloth can be done by simply using an over-cloth placed so both cloths are seen—especially pretty on a round table. My friend Clare Stewart taught me that gathering a tablecloth in the center with a rubber band will create a pleated effect. For this the cloth must be slightly larger than usual so when the center is gathered, the hem will still reach the floor. This treatment will result in a knot in the center of the table that must be covered by a heavy centerpiece, and it will work best when the tablecloth is of lightweight material. It is only suitable for a buffet or serving table.

Create swags along the edges of a table by holding the bottom hem of the cloth in your hand, gathering material as you move up toward the table, and then pinning it in place. A bow of contrasting or matching material will cover the pinning job. The use of an undercloth is important when using this technique. A similar effect can be produced using a garland. Fresh garland materials must be light in weight, such as sprengerii or smilax. Artificial materials are excellent for this treatment. Attach the roping by using straight pins underneath the cloth.

Wrapping a square or rectangular table as a big Christmas present is an easy decorative effect. This looks best when the table cloth reaches the floor. Use a wide ribbon, 3″ to 5″, attaching it with straight pins underneath the cloth in several places, or use double-face adhesive tape to hold the ribbon in place. Make big bows with streamers falling towards the hem for one or two corners. Attach them with pins.

A table looks dramatic and glamorous with a few sprinklings of shiny sequins scattered across the top of a solid color cloth. Place a crystal clear plastic cloth over the top to cover the sequins. This kind of very clear plastic cloth is usually available through display stores or stores specializ-

Corner buffet placement, table against wall

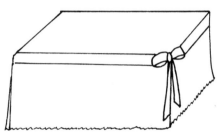

Off center on round table

Table wrapped as a package, flatten the bow

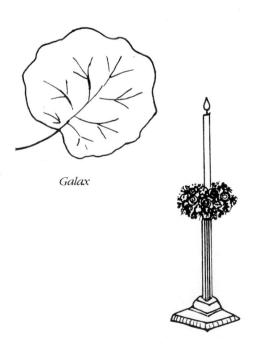

Galax

ing in tent rentals. Great for New Year's Eve!

For a very special holiday gathering of family or friends, use a solid-color tablecloth on which all the guests are invited to sign their names. Provide a selection of fabric markers in a wide range of colors. Fabric paints in tubes for use with a brush may inspire your guests to new levels of creativity. Date the cloth and it will become an heirloom. You must be sure to have a sheet of plastic or something similar underneath during the decorating in the event of leaks.

A cloth constructed from fresh galax leaves is especially pretty for a round dessert table. Begin with an old sheet, dropcloth, or even a plastic cloth cut to fit the table. After trying it on the table for size, spread the cloth out on the floor. Trim the stems from the galax leaves and dab each one with hot glue. Then, beginning in the center of the cloth, fit them closely together and press the first row of leaves into place. For the succeeding rows, center each new leaf between two leaves in the row before, like shingles on a roof. Continue to cover the cloth with the leaves, overlapping each new row. Be sure to press each leaf firmly in place. Finish the center neatly with an extra row of leaves if necessary. When the cloth is completely covered and the leaves firmly in place, gently move it from the floor to the table. Stand by to accept compliments.

Making an entire cloth of galax leaves is very time-consuming, unless you have help. A short cut would be to cover only the top of the table, or simply use a square over-cloth , or runner in the center. Or you could make galax leaf place mats. To do this, cut circles from old plastic place mats or pieces of white posterboard. For a 16″ round mat, cut a circle of the base material with a 12″ diameter. Glue galax leaves onto this base just as you would for the tablecloth, except that for a place mat you should begin with the outside edge, having the first row of leaves extend about two inches over the edge of the mat, and work toward the center. A trio of leaves will cover the center. I made my placemats with artificial galax leaves, and they have been re-used many times and are easily cleaned with a damp sponge.

I enjoy using placemats on my table so I can see the beautiful polished wood. Placemats in the right fabric can be as elegant as a tablecloth. Lace, embroidered cut-work, and linen are all lovely. With placemats on the table, I use serving dishes on the sideboard.

The use of candles makes a table setting more important. Use only high-quality, smokeless, dripless candles and have the flames either well above or below eye level. Freezing candles will make them burn longer.

Candles can be decorated by using small candle rings around the base. These are basically very small garlands made of small stems of foliage, baby's breath, and tiny flowers wired together with fine wire, their ends hooked together. They must be constructed a day ahead of time and refrigerated in sealed plastic bags to keep them fresh. If silk flowers are used, they will look better if real greens are added. Candle garlands made of dried materials—tiny nuts and pinecones, or even pretty Christmas beads—can be made months ahead of time.

Another way to decorate a candle is to create a ring to fit around the base. Cut a 3″ circle of posterboard with a one inch hole in the center for the candle and glue tiny decorations into place around the ring with white craft glue or a hot glue gun. The posterboard should be covered

completely. Canella berries, tiny pinecones, pistachio nuts, even dried flowers could all be used. The dimensions of the ring can be changed to fit an individual candle or candleholder. For safety reasons, candles should never be allowed to burn into a candle ring.

Assorted hard fruits and vegetables used as candleholders are appealing on the dinner table. Simply carve a hole in the top of the fruit or vegetable to accommodate the candle. Be careful cutting because if the hole is too big the candle will wobble, and the candle itself must not be too high or the whole decoration will topple over. When using these fruit or vegetable holders on a table cloth, a piece of Oasis double-sided tape placed under the fruit will help to hold them steady.

A group of assorted sizes and shapes of candleholders makes an attractive centerpiece and it is simple to arrange. The group will be more interesting if the holders do not match, but they should all be made of the same material. Use enough candle-sticks to be effective. The candles should all be the same color, but the heights should vary.

Votive lights, or little tea lights as they are sometimes called, are available everywhere. They are short, round candles inside small glass holders that are safe to use almost anywhere. They are often used as highlights in a large design.

After the tablecloth and centerpiece have been chosen, it is time to consider the individual place settings. Napkin rings add a festive touch. If you feel energetic, you can make individual evergreen wreaths to encircle each napkin—a take home gift for each guest. One of the prettiest napkin rings I use is one which holds fresh flowers in water. They are available from florist and table design shops. I place one above each plate, instead of to the left side where the napkin is usually found. When all the little rings are filled, they make a delightful addition of fresh flowers to the table.

Apple Candleholder

The garnishing of serving platters is important, also. Try using fresh vegetable garnishes with parsley to make little bouquets. Pretty fruit slices make a mouth-watering enhancer. I like to use flowers on platters. Small arrangements in little cups anchored to the center of a serving tray with floral clay or double-stick tape make the whole dish come alive. Do not use poisonous berries such as mistletoe or yew on food platters. Artificial berries can be skillfully tucked into fresh greens for a touch of color. Curly kale leaves enhance the presentation of food on a platter. Study how the caterers do it at the next party you attend. A trip to the supermarket will give you many more ideas.

Table favors come in many forms. They can be small individual gifts, tiny baskets of greens, or miniature boxes of candy. Trim each favor to complement the overall table setting. I love having favors at Christmas. I have used small gold boxes topped with a gold and white ribbon holding a small silk rose, with two pieces of chocolate candy inside—just right for after dinner. Tiny boxes are available in many bright colors as well as silver and gold. Glassine bags can hold a small favor and be trimmed with pretty ribbons. My friend, Dale Balfour, gives a large buffet dinner every Christmas Eve using a gingerbread house as a centerpiece. Each guest is given a gingerbread person with his or her own name in icing. We always look forward to these special cookies.

OPEN KISSING BALL

Roll of medium #20 wire and wire clippers

Ball 8" to 10" diameter, or a filled balloon

White craft glue

Green sheet moss

Dried or silk flowers, leaves, berries, cones

Roll of fine #30 wire for flowers

Ribbons

Hot glue gun

Mistletoe, real or artificial

To make the frame for an open kissing ball, use an 8" to 10" ball or an inflated balloon as a pattern and guide. Make a circle of sturdy wire around the ball or balloon and twist the wire together after a single circle has been made. Remove the ball or balloon. Carefully fashion a second length of wire into another circle like the first one. Place it inside the first circle and wire them together at the top and bottom. Repeat for a third time, adding this circle to the other two to form an openwork ball with six sections. All the circles should be firmly wired together where they meet at the top and bottom.

Cover the wire framework of the ball with craft glue and press small pieces of moss into place around each wire. Let dry. Proceed to glue or wire decorations of silk or dried flowers, leaves, cones, or berries onto the moss-covered frame. Small velvet leaves can be added.

Make a loop of ribbon to hang the kissing ball at the top by tying the ribbon under the ribs at the top of the ball and slipping the knot underneath. A touch of hot glue on the knot will keep it from slipping.

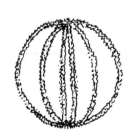

Make a few graceful streamers for the bottom. They may be wired to the bottom of the ball or hot glued into place. Tuck a piece of mistletoe into the ball and hang.

As a variation, a small Oasis Iglu can be wired into the center bottom of the open ball. The floral foam inside the cage must be wet before it is put into place. Fill the foam with fresh flowers spilling out in all directions!

THE CHRISTMAS TREE

The celebration of Christmas brings to mind many kinds of decorations, but none so traditional and important as the Christmas tree. When the tree is large, it becomes the focal point in the area where it is displayed. Whether your tree is large or small, make it a joyous display, using ornaments selected for the scale of the tree.

Personally, I like a tree to reflect the personality of those it serves. There is no right or wrong way to decorate a Christmas tree, whether it is done with magnificent antique ornaments handed down from generations long gone, or simple ornaments cut from paper. On our own tree we use a blend of ornaments from the past and present, some inherited, some given by friends, and some made by the children when they were small. We remember a time, person, or event connected with many of them and, when we trim the tree each year, all the memories come forth, fresh and bright.

The placement of the tree in a room determines the way it is decorated. A tree placed in a corner needs far less decorating than a free-standing one. If a tree is placed in front of a window, all the light flooding through the tree must be considered. A very full or thick-branched tree should be chosen for this location. Extra branches may have to be wired into the center of the tree to make it appear full. Additional ornaments, garlands, or icicles may be needed. Bunches of fresh baby's breath can be inserted into open spaces. The baby's breath will dry beautifully in position.

Make certain the tree is steady, even if you have to wire it to nails placed in the baseboards; and be sure the tree has a good source of water. Check the level of the water every day so your tree will not be a fire hazard.

Examine the lights to make certain they are all working before you put them on the tree. Hang the ornaments after the lights are in place.

Finally, if you care to do so, a skirt can be placed around the base of the tree. This can be anything from an embroidered, quilted, or needle-pointed circular skirt to a plain piece of fabric fluffed around the bottom. I have seen short pieces of fencing used around the bottom of the tree, as well as groupings of living plants. If you place your tree inside a wooden planter, it must be done before any decorations are added. Trees in planters look as if they are still alive.

A living tree to be planted outside after Christmas must have the planting hole prepared before the ground freezes. The hole should be well watered and filled with leaves before Christmas. As long as the tree is inside the house, keep its ball of earth moist. Within a few days after Christmas, the tree should be moved to its prepared hole. Water it well. We have had several live trees. Some of them lived and some did not. The conservation-minded may enjoy knowing that a live tree will help the environment, but a cut tree can also also help the environment if, instead being put out for the trash collector, it is taken to a recycling center to be turned into mulch. Some recycling centers reward donors with a bag of mulch and a pine seedling.

SOME THOUGHTS ON TREE TRIMMING

Try decorating with tiny white lights and ornaments all one color, such as gold or silver.

Eliminate lights and tie bunches of dried flowers on the tree.

Use only bows and multi-colored lights. Small styrofoam balls could be wrapped with identical ribbon and added. This would be particularly effective using an informal checked ribbon, or lovely embroidered silk ribbons.

Use fresh flowers inserted into vials of water tied to the branches with pretty ribbons.

Festoon the tree with garlands of popcorn and cranberries. Add popcorn balls in glassine bags tied with pretty ribbon.

Make an origami tree using an assortment of different papers.

Try polished cookie cutters tied on with bright ribbon—especially attractive for a kitchen or family room.

Fill tiny baskets with small candies and tie them to the branches. Christmas visitors can take home a little favor.

If you are a collector of old toys, attach some of the smaller ones to the tree and pile the larger ones at the base to show off your collection.

A tree with a multitude of collected figures of any kind would be interesting. St. Nicholas figures would be wonderful.

A tree for cooks! Bake delicious sugar and ginger cookies with a hole punched in the top before they are cooked, and hang them for children to enjoy.

Trim styrofoam balls with gaily-colored yarn and sequins. Place a few crepe paper pinatas at the base of the tree.

Flock the tree with white "snow" and dust it with glitter.

Stuff the crevices of the tree with preserved baby's breath and hang styrofoam balls that have been rolled in white craft glue and potpourri.

Use traditional ornaments, blending all sizes, shapes, and colors. Add a few new ones every year and enjoy the old and new together. There are a thousand ways to trim a tree. Make yours personal, a reflection of your heritage and interests.

To illustrate that the Hogarth curve design really is a transposed wreath, the same design is shown both ways, as a curve and then repositioned to form a wreath.

HOGARTH CURVE CENTERPIECE

Oasis plastic wreath frame
Sabre saw with plastic-cutting blade
Tube of Red Devil paste adhesive
Wet Oasis to fill the frame
Sheet of plastic to protect table

Assorted fresh evergreen sprigs, 5″ long
Assorted fresh fruit or flowers
Magnolia leaves

The amount of material used for this design is determined by the size of the wreath frame.

Cut the plastic wreath frame in half with the electric saw. Create a small barrier at each cut end with the paste adhesive. Make the barrier as deep as the side walls of the wreath frame. Work the adhesive into place with your finger tips to ensure a tight seal. Let it dry completely, about two days. Test the watertight seal by filling the frame with water. If there are no leaks, fill the frame with wet floral foam. If the frame is not completely watertight, add more adhesive to fill any small spaces that are leaking.

Work on this design in the kitchen so escaping water will do no harm. Position the two pieces of wreath frame into an S-shape, and fill the frame completely with evergreens. Complete the sides first and then the top by pushing the stems into position at slightly varying angles. Two of the ends, the ones that will be joined together, should not be heavily covered with greens. On the ends that will not meet, the greens should cover the foam.

Last to be placed in position are the fruits or flowers. Arrange one or the other, or perhaps both, along the curve working them as close to the foam as possible. Fruits should be impaled on wooden picks to hold them steady.

When it is time to carry the design to the dining table, prepare the area where the design will be placed by covering it with plastic to protect the table. Move the design in sections, placing them carefully on the plastic. Make certain no water is escaping. After the design is in place, slide individual magnolia leaves under the design to enhance the edges and cover the plastic.

This design would be just as pretty done with evergreens and Christmas ornaments. The ornaments will be easier to work with if they are pre-wired for easy insertion into the foam. A Hogarth curve design of dried materials would also be effective.

If you choose to execute this in dried materials, the ends of the wreath frame do not need to be sealed off. In place of Oasis, fill the frame with Sahara. A dried design will need a great quantity of materials; keep this in mind when either purchasing the materials or drying your own.

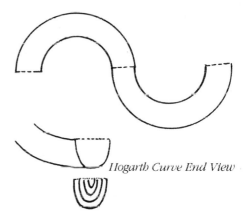

Hogarth Curve End View

Suggested materials for a Hogarth curve.

Fruit - apples, pears, oranges, lemons, limes, grapes, kumquats, clusters of cherries, tangerines, pomegranates, marzipan strawberries.

Flowers - camellias, roses, alstroemeria, statice, lilies, carnations, chrysanthemums, freesia, baby's breath, nerines, paperwhite narcissus, anemonies, ranunculas

Foliage - magnolia, holly, pine, fir, ivy, leucothe, boxwood, camellia, fern, myrtle, ruskus

Trims - nandina berries, pepper berries, china berries, popcorn tree berries, pinecones, walnuts, pecans, velvet ribbon, holly berries, tree ornaments

Dried materials - poppy heads, lotus pods, Queen Anne's lace, strawflowers, cockscomb, okra pods, rosehips, roses, pinecones, baby's breath, dried mushrooms, gomfrina, magnolia pods, thistle, wheat stalks, yarrow, hydrangea, eucalyptus, lunaria, any dried flower from the garden.

FRESH FLOWER WREATH

Large round plastic tray, 16"
  diameter
Three to four blocks of wet floral
  foam

Four dozen assorted fresh flowers
Fresh greens from the garden or
  two to three purchased bunches
Candles and candleholders, optional

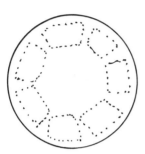

This wreath does not hang. Lay chunks of wet floral foam around the outside edge of a large round tray. The chunks of foam should almost touch each other. Or, use the convenient new wreath form now available from Oasis. This is a reinforced green plastic frame filled with Oasis. All you have to do is soak it thoroughly. First, insert greens sparingly into the foam all the way around, leaving open spaces throughout for the flowers. The greens should extend over the edges of the tray. The greens on the inside of the circle should help camouflage the plastic tray, if you are using one. I like to use fresh variegated pittisporum, pine, holly, and baker fern for a good variety of shape, size, and texture, as well as color.

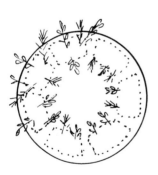

Next insert the fresh flowers you have chosen. They could all be of one variety or a mixture. I like the combination of alstroemeria, miniature carnations, freesia, snowflake chrysanthemums, and roses. Fresh white statice is a good filler, as are fresh baby's breath and wax flowers. These are all standard flowers, readily available. The stems of the flowers should be cut very short, no more than 3" or 4", and the flower heads should be nestled close to the wreath to keep the shape circular and compact. Flowers should cover the inside and outside edges as well as the top of the wreath.

When the wreath has been completed, add a cluster of candles in the center; or, perhaps, a single pillar candle. Candles can be inserted directly into the wreath, but only if you use the candle adapters. Do not try to put a candle directly into the foam without these adapters because the candles will mash the foam so it cannot hold the candle firmly. Instead of candles, perhaps a piece of sculpture could be used in the center.

This flower wreath can be used for any season using whatever flowers are available at the time. I made a sensational one during the summer using assorted zinnias, daisies, and marigolds from my garden. Ageratum and small garden begonias are good fillers for this design. Eliminate too many heavy greens in the summer because annuals themselves have plenty of leaves to provide the filling-in. Should you have any open spaces, tuck in little bits of damp sphagnum moss.

An attractive and less expensive all-green wreath could be created, eliminating the use of flowers altogether. Simply use enough assorted greens to fill the entire wreath and insert Christmas ornaments wired to floral picks into the greens for color.

EPERGNE

An epergne, which is a dinner table decoration of bowls or vases supported on branches, provides a dramatic and elegant centerpiece rising above a table setting. If you do not have one, and most of us do not, you can create the feeling of one by using a three or five branch candelabra with a raised center candleholder. Small silver or crystal bowls can be fixed to the candleholders by using either floral adhesive or double-sided tape. Instead of bowls, Oasis O'dapters could be used in the side holders, and a larger bowl placed on the central top holder. The center bowl should be larger than the others. The candelabra is ready to be decorated as if it were an epergne!

The dishes of an epergne can be filled with fresh flowers and greens or fruits of the season, candies, nuts, or Christmas ornaments. It is not necessary to fill them all with identical materials, but there should be some continuity of design either by repetition of materials or with the use of draped ribbons to visually carry the eye around the display. Color coordination is important. Variation in the tones of a single color is often more pleasing than a melange of colors. A combination that looks well together is: small pears, greenish-yellow apples, limes, frosted white grapes, and green and white wandering Jew. Or try kumquats, tangerines, lemons, white grapes and ivy vine; or plums, cherries, red grapes and purple wandering Jew.

A pineapple is often used for the central, most prominent, position in an epergne because it is the symbol of hospitality. If you can find the very small decorative pineapples, they might be incorporated into the side dishes of the epergne, but only if the dishes are large enough to accommodate them in addition to other material.

If you use add freshly-cut vines they will have to be placed in small tubes of water before being inserted into the design. Every day the arrangement is in use, the tubes should be removed and refilled with fresh water to keep the vines fresh. I like to add sprigs of evergreens, also, to fill empty spaces.

When using an epergne, a feeling of restrained elegance should prevail. Do not overload the epergne with too many small, insignificant items. Avoid a cluttered look. Roses, freesia, small lilies, and smilax are lovely together, but there are countless combinations. Chrysanthemums are long-lasting flowers that stay fresh for many days, as are alstroemeria and wax flowers. When using fresh materials in an epergne, the mechanics must include wet floral foam to keep the materials fresh. The foam should be secured to the bowl by an anchor pin held in place with floral adhesive.

Later, when the candelabra is no longer being used as an epergne all traces of adhesive can be removed with Ronsonol lighter fluid.

FRESH FLOWER TREE
Illustrated on the back cover

1 1/2 bricks of wet floral foam
Green floral adhesive tape
Plate, about 8" diameter
Floral foam spike
Floral clay
Slender dowel, or 3 #18 wires
  bound together
Knife
Clippers
Fresh flowers, approximately two
dozen assorted stems of flowers
for one tree—carnations, mini-
carnations, baby's breath, freesias,
roses, alstroemeria, rubrum lilies
with a few buds, snowflake
chrysanthemums
Fresh greens, a handful of stems of
each variety per tree—fern, ruskus,
pittisporum
Damp sphagnum moss

Make this tree the day before you plan to use it; so, if you need more flowers, you have time to purchase them. Fix a floral foam spike to the plate with floral clay and push an upended brick of floral foam onto the spike. Place the half brick on top. Insert a slender dowel, or 3 #18 straight wires which have been taped together with floral tape, down through the center of the two bricks, holding them together. Cut off any extra wire or dowel that is exposed. Trim the foam to a tree shape by slicing off the edges of the top block. Bring green floral adhesive tape up from under the plate, over the top of the foam, and back down under the plate, sticking it to itself underneath. Repeat this procedure on the other side of the tree. This will hold the tree steady on the plate while you are working on it.

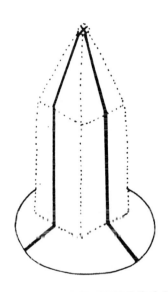

Begin placing your flowers into the wet foam by establishing the top flower height first. Place a few flowers around the bottom of the tree to give the idea of the width at the base. Insert flowers at various levels going up the tree, using flower stems of varying lengths, from 3" to 6", in order to keep all the flower heads at the same level. Periodically insert some greens along with the flowers. If there are spaces where you have deliberately not inserted flowers to keep the design airy and loose, use small pieces of damp moss to cover any foam which may be visible.

For a variation of this tree with the same basic mechanics, use five dozen standard-size carnations all of one color—red, white, pink—and pack them solidly into the tree, using very little greenery. If some of the carnations are not open, you can usually ease them open with your fingers by gently spreading the the petals around in a circular fashion. Allowing partially opened flowers to stand in warm water will also help them open more fully.

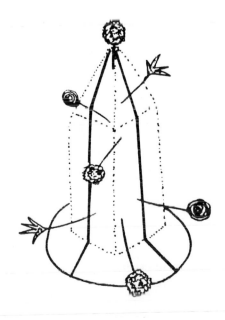

I have also made this tree using Sahara and red silk carnations which, of course, do not die and can be used again and again.

Fern

Small protea, flat

Hydrangea

Bayberry

A CHRISTMAS MIRROR

Mirror or special craft mirror purchased with a styrofoam frame molded in place
White craft glue or hot glue gun
Nuts. pods, cones, deer moss, dried berries
Tiny dried flowers, pressed fern, sheet moss
Whole spices
Small ornaments or wooden fruit, shells, toys
Artificial holly and greens

Begin this project well in advance of Christmas for a versatile and long-lasting centerpiece for your dining room table. It can also be used on a glass cocktail table or with the addition of a hanger in back as a hanging wall mirror.

For this project either recycle a mirror from the attic, or go to a glass and mirror shop and have them cut a mirror to your specification. Ask the mirror cutter to bevel the sharp edges. Cover the back of the mirror completely with felt to protect table surfaces. There are round mirrors available already mounted in a green styrofoam frame on which to build a design. These are wonderful.

Collect all sorts of cones, pods, acorns and other nuts during the fall and bake them on a cookie sheet in the oven at 225° for half an hour to finish off any little creatures that might be hiding inside the nuts or pods.

Next decide if you like the natural look of the pods and nuts, or whether you would prefer a more polished look. I like the polished effect and so I paint my collection by laying all of the nuts and pods out on a newspaper and giving them a quick spray of glossy wood-tone paint, or I dip them in a bowl of liquid brown shoe polish to intensify the browns of the natural materials and prevent fading.

Before you glue the materials in place, lay out a pattern with the nuts and pods all along the edges of the mirror. This way you can see which pieces look compatible next to one another. When you have found a design that is pleasing, place a small amount of glue on the mirror and press the materials into place. As you work along the edges of the mirror, every so often include a small piece of deer moss or green moss in the design. It will give a nice change of color and texture.

Deer moss is lovely to use; it has a silvery gray color. If it is dry when you find or purchase it, moisten it to make it soft and easy to use, tear off small pieces the size you need, and when it dries it will become quite hard again. Small pieces of pressed fern can also be worked into the design. They are very delicate which relieves some of the heaviness of the larger cones and pods.

Dried flowers add a bit of color and they are perfectly in keeping with the other materials. Cream-colored preserved baby's breath is another filler which is light and airy and does not shed too easily. Just make sure it has been glycerinized, not dried. A dab of glue will hold it in place. All you want are the flowers so make the stems very short. A few artificial berries tucked into the design add color. Cinnamon sticks, vanilla stalks, cloves, and cinnamon-coated nuts (whole nuts covered with glue and rolled in cinnamon) emit a light fragrance if used in the design. They also add an interesting change of shape.

Another version of this mirror can be assembled by using an assort-

ment of shiny Christmas balls glued into place around the edges. Do not use the molded styrofoam form for this design. Artificial holly, ivy and long-needled pine is available which can be used in conjunction with the glittery ornaments. This makes a dazzling centerpiece for the holidays. When using the ornaments, no moss is required as the artificial greenery is enough. A sprinkling of glitter or artificial snow here and there across the mirror could add a finishing touch. Add a snowman or jolly Santa figure in the center.

If you live near the ocean, a mirror surrounded by lovely seashells is appropriate. The shells can be used in their natural creamy-peachy-pink state or they can be painted with gold leaf for an entirely different appearance. Glue them in place around the edges of the mirror. They will make a more interesting design if they are placed in various positions— inside each other, spread out, or upside down. Sprinkle a little fine sand or gravel over a dab of glue in the spaces where there are no shells. To achieve the best design, position the material around the mirror first, and when you are satisfied that nothing could be improved by rearranging, glue everything in place permanently. Remove excess sand or gravel with a paint brush to keep it from creeping off the mirror onto your table. If you need additional material, select some fresh statice which can dry in position. For a touch of green, I would suggest something in a pale color that would be in harmony with the sea. Small tendrils of dried or artificial ivy could also be included but use a size of ivy leaf in proportion to the size of the shells. The final addition of a strand of pearls entwined throughout the shells will add a soft lustrous glow.

When your mirror is complete, in the center place several glass votive candleholders with fresh galax leaves bound on with strands of raffia.

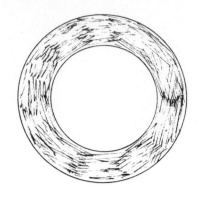

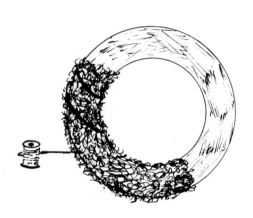

MOSS WREATH ON A STRAW FRAME

A straw wreath frame may be used for this project in whatever way it comes—plain or wrapped with green plastic. Soak the moss and squeeze out the excess water. Place pieces of moss onto the wreath frame and wrap the moss securely to the frame with either fine wire or fishing line. Any fragments of moss not tied into place can be attached with fern pins. When the wreath has been completely covered, wrap the end of the wire around a fern pin and insert the pin into the wreath.

If the moss is not a uniformly attractive color, it may be tinted with a mixture of water and several drops each of green and yellow food coloring. Test the color and adjust it before using on the wreath. Do this only if the wreath will not be exposed to rain because food color is not permanent and will definitely run if it gets wet.

Because the purpose of making this design is to achieve a mossy wreath, use only a minimum of trim. Sprigs of evergreen can be attached easily with fern pins while the moss is still damp. However it is best to attach ribbons when the moss is dry. Small Oasis Iglus can be attached to the wreath by inserting fern pins through their side tabs so materials that require water may be used. Dried materials may be inserted directly through the moss into the straw, or they may be hot-glued into place.

SMALL MOSS-COVERED ANIMALS

Inexpensive small plastic animals from the variety store can be transformed easily into attractive decorations by covering them with an overcoat of green moss.

Select a small plastic animal suitable in size and type for your purpose and cover it with a coat of craft glue. Press small bits of dried moss into place, covering the plastic completely. To get a smooth coat, use pieces of moss that are all of the same thickness. After the glue and moss have dried, clip away any excess strands of moss that are making the animal shaggy.

If the moss you use is brown and dry-looking, it can be tinted a pretty green color by mixing a little green and yellow food coloring with water in a spray bottle. Experiment, drop by drop, with the colors until you are happy with the shade. One cup of water with several drops of each color is a good starting point. Commercial florist tints are available if you do not want to mix your own.

A pretty garland of dried flowers around the neck can be added. Dried pot-pourri can be substituted for the moss. The procedure is the same. These moss covered animals can be used with flower arrangement compositions at any time of the year.

BASKETS

There are many ways baskets can be used for Christmas, from very tiny baskets used for favors on the dining room table to a large floor basket used as a container for firewood or even the Christmas tree itself. Basket trims can be whimsical or intricate. They can be stained, painted, or covered with fabric or moss. Nuts, pods, cones, real or artificial flowers can be affixed. Baskets can be beribboned, mossed over, or covered with candy canes or cinnamon sticks. Only your imagination sets the limit.

Pleated Ribbon

The simplest way to brighten an old basket is to stain it or paint it if the weave is still intact. If the weave is damaged, the basket will have to be covered with moss or fabric.

Before painting a basket, make sure it is clean and free of all particles of dirt hiding in the weave. A basket can usually be washed and scrubbed with a brush, but let it dry completely before painting it. Select a vibrant color and begin by turning the basket upside down, painting the underside first. When that is dry, turn it over and paint the inside, outside, and top. A pair of disposable plastic gloves is invaluable while doing any kind of painting at close range. Do not try to cover the surface of the basket with one coat of paint. It is better to use several light coats which will also eliminate any problem with drips. Enamel paint especially must be used with a light hand. For repeat coats, apply paint in the opposite direction. By doing this, you will be able to see any areas that were not covered by the first coat. Hang the basket to dry on a hook.

Pinecone Covered

Baskets do not have to be red or green for Christmas. Paint one to harmonize with the color of your home or try a contrasting color. Christmas enjoys a full range of color. Try dark, rich purple trimmed with silver ribbon, or paint a silver basket and add a burgundy ribbon. Burgundy and dusty rose are lovely together. When painting a dark basket white, first paint the basket silver which will cover the dark color. Several coats of white will then give you a finished basket. The first coat or two may look gray, but continue with the next coats and it will be fine.

Moss-covered

Moss-covered baskets are charming and woodsy in feeling. As a rule I cover only the outside of a basket, but you may need to cover the inside of a basket if it is only going to hold a few pinecones or wrapped candy canes. If the basket is to be filled or used with a liner, it is not necessary to line the inside.

To line the outside of a basket with moss, first clean it thoroughly and paint the inside. Next, try to remove as much dirt as possible from the moss so it will adhere. Slather craft glue, linoleum paste, or hot glue all around the outside of the basket and press the moss into place. When the moss is dry, excess pieces can be snipped away. If a basket has a handle, cover the top as well as the underside of the handle with glue. Press moss onto the glue and reinforce by wrapping the handle with very fine wire or fishing line that will be almost invisible when complete. A streamer of ribbon on each side of the basket is a final touch.

Select any new basket with a specific purpose in mind. I usually recommend to my customers in the shop that they choose a large basket rather than a small one. An empty basket will not look much larger when it is filled. Always take a basket home "on approval" to see how it looks in place.

Dried Material in Cage

Open

Wire Wall Basket

A wire wall basket used for summer flowers can be put to use at Christmas as a wall or door decoration; two of them could be used on either side of a door, or hanging on the door shutters if you have them.

If you choose to make this kind of arrangement in a hanging basket, you will need to use more material and make it attractive all around. Wicker baskets can also be filled with greens. Simply eliminate the moss lining, except for what is needed to hold the liner in place. A wicker handle does not need to be covered, but the addition of a bow may appeal to you.

Empty and clean a basket you have on hand, or use a new one. Cover the inside of the basket with Spanish moss or green sheet moss. Moss is easier to work with if it is damp. Fit the basket with some kind of liner. If a plastic bag is used roll down the extra plastic and tuck it inside. Fill the liner with wet floral foam that is higher than the edge of the basket. The height of the foam is important so material can be inserted up into the foam to look as if it is flowing out of the basket. Stuff more moss around the liner if necessary to hold it steady in the basket. Fill the basket by inserting evergreens and, if the weather is mild, flowers. I do not advise artificial flowers if the weather is freeezing. Decorations should be believable. Cones, berries, and pods are bright and cheerful for Christmas.

A wide basket deep enough to hold a large clay pot can be filled with blooming Christmas plants. Use a large plastic bag for a liner. Fold down the excess and tuck it inside the basket. Place the largest plant or plants inside first. Spoon in either wood chips or perlite to raise the height of the bottom for smaller pots so all the foliage and flowers will be raised to the correct height. Cover any spaces with damp moss so the overall appearance is green. Trim the handle of the basket with a pretty Christmas bow.

SMALL NUT AND POD DECORATIONS

Styrofoam balls or cones
Brown floral paint suitable for
  styrofoam
Narrow ribbon
Fern pins

Assorted small nuts, pods, and
  cones
Hot glue gun
Glossy wood-tone spray paint or
  brown liquid shoe polish

Delightful and unique Christmas decorations and gifts can be made quickly by gluing cones and pods onto styrofoam forms.

Dry a selection of small cones, pods, and nuts in the oven set to 225° for twenty minutes, then let them cool. Spray them with glossy wood-tone paint or dip them in brown liquid shoe polish.

Paint a white or green styrofoam form brown, using paint specifically made for styrofoam. Many paints will cause styrofoam to disintegrate so be sure to use the right kind of paint. Let it dry.

To make a kissing ball, first divide a styrofoam ball into four sections with ribbon by wrapping the ribbon around the ball in both directions and securing it with U-shaped wire pins touched with hot glue. Before pinning the ribbon into place at the top and bottom, give the ribbon a little pinch to make it narrower at these points.

Plan a pattern of nuts and pods in each section of the kissing ball. Then dab a little hot glue on each piece of material and press it in place onto the ball. Hold it steady until set. Build your design from the bottom up, fitting the cones and pods closely together. If you have a few small open spaces when the ball is finished, you can fill them with small pieces of moss or small pinecone scales glued into place.

When all the sections are completely filled in, make a loop of ribbon and affix it to the top of the ball with a fern pin coated with glue. Make streamers for the bottom of the ball by pinching loops of ribbon together and attaching them with a fern pin.

If you want a bow with the streamers, make loop of ribbon with a streamer at one end, push a fern pin through the ribbon to hold the loop, make three more loops, pushing the same fern pin through the base each time the loop ends (it is done this way, pushing the fern pin in at each turn, because it would be very difficult to push the fern pin through all the loops at one time). When there are four loops, allow another streamer to fall and cut off the ribbon. Push the bow (formed by the loops) and the streamers into the bottom of the ball with the fern pin. Add a little dab of hot glue on the fern pin to hold it in place.

A small tree of nuts and pods is made in the same way—by gluing the material onto a brown-painted styrofoam cone. Since the tree will not have to be divided into sections with ribbon, the only design consideration is to use the larger material at the bottom decreasing in size as you move upward. Save the smallest most perfect cone for the very top. An attractive base for the tree can be made by gluing green sheet moss onto a tuna fish can.

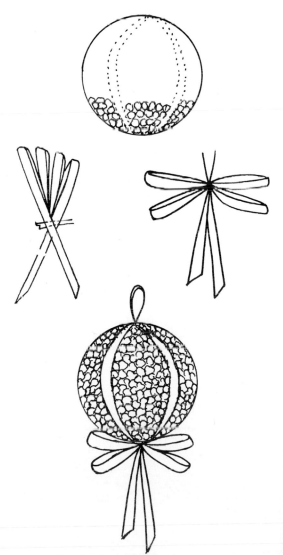

SUNNY O'NEIL'S SWEET GUM BALL TEDDY BEAR

Four blocks of floral foam
Linoleum paste, dark brown
Market bag full of sweet gum balls
Toothpicks or #18 straight wires
   and floral tape

Two shiny black buttons without
   holes
Black felt
Ribbon for bow tie
Glossy wood-tone paint, optional

Sweet Gum Ball

Many years ago I took a course in pressed flower arrangements from Sunny O'Neil at her home in Maryland. Her house was filled with antiques and Victoriana, lovely bouquets of dried flowers, wreaths, fanciful Christmas decorations, and a marvelous sweet gum bear! I asked for directions to make him and Mrs. O'Neil had a book available which I bought and took home to study. The bear has been a part of our Christmas ever since. I have made bears for the church bazaar, bears for family, and bears for friends. Now, with Mrs. O'Neil's gracious consent, I can share the directions, from her booklet, *Sunny O'Neil's Favorite Christmas Decorations,* with you.

Gather at least one full market bag of wonderful, prickly, sweet gum balls. You can see them in the late fall hanging like cherries from the bare limbs of the trees; or, if you are lucky, they have fallen to the ground. I suggest wearing gloves to gather them because they are very prickly to handle. If you live in an area where the sweet gum tree does not grow, ask your florist to try to get some for you.

To make the bear, place a block of dry floral foam on end. Cut a second block in half and trim all the edges from one of the halves. Glue the trimmed half-block to the top of the up-ended block with linoleum paste, first strengthening the joint by inserting several toothpicks. Or, bind three lengths of #18 wire together with floral tape, cut the wires to a suitable length, and use the bound wires as picks. I have been more successful using wire because it can be cut longer for more support. The half-block becomes the head and the whole block becomes the body of the bear.

Cut two pieces of foam for the legs, 5″ long by 1 1/2″ square. Cut a notch in one end of each leg piece so it will fit snugly against the body. Trim the edges, insert the toothpicks or wires, and glue into place. Do the arms in the same way. Now you will see that he needs a nose, two ears, and some fattening.

The nose should be 3″ wide, 3 1/2″ high, and protrude from the head two inches. Round it off and attach it with picks and glue.

The two ear pieces should be 4″ wide by 3″ high by 3/4″ thick. Trim them into circles, fit them with picks, and attach them to the top corners of the head.

The additional pieces to fatten his head are 3″ high, 1″ square. Trim the edges and attach them with glue and picks.

To plump out his body, add a trimmed piece to each side that is 4″ high and 1 1/2″ square. The piece for the stomach should be 4″ high, 3 1/2″ wide, and 2″ thick before it is shaped. It does not matter if the measurements are varied a little, but they can serve as a guide. Allow the frame to dry for 24 hours.

Working from the bottom up, cover small sections of the bear at a

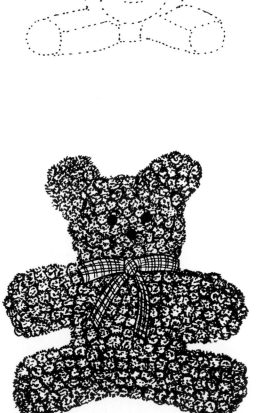

time with linoleum paste. Push individual sweet gum balls into the paste-covered floral foam as firmly as possible. I work the bear in sections—underside of the legs first, then the tops of the legs, sides of the legs last. Finish the underside of the body, working up to the middle of the stomach. Let this dry, overnight at least.

Do the next section the same way, finishing the stomach, doing under the arms, up the chest and the back of the head. Again, let it dry overnight. When the bear is drying, he may have to lie in strange positions to keep the gum balls from slipping off.

Finish by gluing the rest of the arms and, finally, the head. Allow the finished bear to dry for at least 24 hours.

I then give mine an all-over spray with a glossy wood-tone paint to give the pods a uniform color and shine. Usually all the pods I gather are slightly different colors of brown, making for a strange looking creature. The paint makes him more attractive to my eye.

Last, add two shiny black buttons for eyes and a piece of black felt cut into a circle for the nose. Attach them with white craft glue or a hot glue gun. Make a bow tie of bright red plaid ribbon for under his chin. Glue a piece of black felt under the bear so the gum balls will not scratch the table surface. I usually display my bear on a glass plate and I tuck freshly-cut holly around him. A very merry bear for Christmas!

DECORATING THE KITCHEN

At Christmas we all spend extra time in the kitchen, so what better room to brighten for the holidays?

Cluster glass jars on the countertop, filling them with Christmas cookies, candies, or even shiny ornaments just for color. Decorate the jars with bright ribbons and tuck in a piece of holly.

Be-ribboned cookie cutters grouped together, but hanging at different heights, are an attractive decoration. To hang any article in the kitchen without putting a hole in the wall, use the kitchen cabinet doors as a backdrop. After attaching a ribbon to the item to be hung, take the ribbon over the top of the cabinet door, and secure it on the inside of the door with tape. This only works with lightweight decorations. If you are uncertain about using tape on the cabinet door, test the tape on a small corner before going forward with the decoration.

A good decoration to hang from a kitchen cabinet door is a cranberry wreath. Round off the edges of a green styrofoam wreath form with a knife, using a sawing motion. Cover the styrofoam with sheet moss held in place with fern pins. The back does not need to be covered with moss. Apply cranberries to the inside edge of the wreath by first inserting the sharp end of a halved toothpick through the moss and into the styrofoam. Top each toothpick with a cranberry. Place the berries close together so very little moss shows. On the top surface, leave a space empty of berries where a bow and fresh greens will go. I usually leave space at the bottom, but it could be on either side, depending on how you plan to hang the wreath. Continue placing toothpicks and berries over the remainder of the wreath. A 10" wreath form will take about two packages of cranberries. Finish the wreath by wiring fresh greens and a bow into the place left bare for them. Hang the wreath by looping a long 2" wide ribbon around the wreath, carrying the ribbon over the top of the cabinet door and taping it on the inside.

Wooden bowls are wonderful containers for apples accented with small sprigs of holly. Apples may be held in place with double-faced adhesive tape.

An apple or lemon tree made in the Williamsburg manner looks festive as a centerpiece on the kitchen table. The Williamsburg Foundation Craft Shop sells the special wooden cones embedded with spikes that make this such an easy decoration to build. A cone will last forever so it is an investment worth making. Other than fruit, the only materials needed are sprigs of green to fill in the spaces between the fruit. Directions accompany the purchase of the cone.

A basket of vegetables can be delightful. Select vegetables of a single color highlighted with vines in vials of water hidden among the vegetables. Try artichokes, asparagus, avocados, limes, broccoli, cucumbers, kale, and brussel sprouts with their leaves slightly opened to form rosettes.

For an attractive basket of breads, use loaves of varying colors and textures, some seeded, some braided, and remember to include a few long bread sticks, unusual crackers, and rolls. Garnish your bread basket with a few stalks of wheat (available through your florist) or rye tied with a checkered ribbon.

Placing a bowlful of clove-studded oranges on the counter is a fragrant way to brighten the kitchen. Plan a design or pattern for each orange and gently score it into the orange skin; then, selecting whole cloves with full heads, press the pointed ends into the flesh of the orange following the pattern. The intricacy of the design will determine how many cloves will be needed. They must be close together to be effective. After the design has been filled in, roll the orange in orris root and spices. Use a small brush to whisk away any spices adhering to the fruit. Make enough of these decorated oranges to highlight a bowl of undecorated fruit.

HINTS

Magnolia leaves can be polished using a little skim milk rubbed on with a piece of cotton.

To get the best effect from holly berries, remove existing leaves which usually cover most berries. Cluster stems of berries together, and add to other stems of holly leaves.

If you cannot locate fern pins, make your own by using short lengths (3" to 4") of #18 wire bent into the shape of a U. Wrap the wire with floral tape before bending it, because a wrapped wire will hold materials to a base better than an unwrapped one.

#22 wire is a good choice for roll wire.

Sweet Gum Ball

Pinecones, pods, and dried materials can easily be painted or glittered. Sweet gum balls can be transformed into large red berries with the application of paint. When gum balls are painted gold and wired onto stiff wires, they can add impact to a contemporary arrangement by jutting out of the design.

Sticks painted or dusted with glitter give unexpected impact when incorporated in green designs. They can also add height and line to an overall design.

There is a Southern tree, commonly called popcorn plant or Chinese tallow tree, *sapium subiferum,* whose branches have clusters of small creamy-white berries that can add attractive touches of natural white color to Christmas designs. Ask your florist to obtain some for you.

Pepper berries and leaves, *schinos molle,* that are grown commercially in California are available in my area in the early fall. The berries are a lovely rose-pink color and they dry beautifully. Try to incorporate some into your Christmas wreaths. The leaves remain on the stems while drying—a definite plus. This is also a pretty material to combine with bay leaves. Another variety of pepper berry from the Brazilian pepper tree *schinos terebinthifolius,* is bright red. This tree grows in Florida and Hawaii. It is also called the Christmas berry tree.

Strings of cranberries can be frosted by dipping them into egg white beaten with a little water before rolling them in granulated sugar. Garlands of cranberries frosted this way are delightful looped through fruit arrangements.

Strings of Popcorn and Cranberries

Holes made in painted wood by staples can be filled with a drop of paint applied directly to the hole with a very fine-tip brush. I fill nail holes with white toothpaste. The toothpaste will act as a spackle, but it is easy to use on the tip of a finger. When dry, it can be re-touched with a drop of matching paint with a fine-tip brush.

Dents in brass containers can often be repaired by covering the dent on the bulging side with a towel and gently hammering the bulge back into shape.

Camellia

Individual leaves which may be too large for a particular design, yet are of the right shape and texture, can be trimmed to size with a pair of sharp scissors by following the general shape of the leaf. The leaves must have substance for this to work; for instance, ivy, galax, camellia, magnolia, iris, hosta, and lily-of-the-valley foliage. A leaf with a bad tip or a hole that is near the edge can still be used if the damaged part is clipped off and the leaf reshaped to the original contour.

Save plastic berry or cherry tomato baskets to use for making your own floral cages. They can be filled with wet or dry floral foam, wired together, and be either impaled on a dowel for a topiary or hung by a ribbon for a kissing ball.

A dusting of cocoa on a too-bright gold candle will tame the color.

Save those large, round plastic trays from the deli. They make wonderful bases for wreaths used on tables or for large low mounded flower arrangements when no container is necessary.

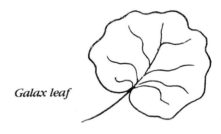

Galax leaf

A burnt match tip rubbed into the cut end of a branch disguises the cut.

Coating a bare branch with glossy wood-tone paint or liquid brown shoe polish gives added depth of color to the branch, but do not do this in a flower show unless the schedule allows it.

A flower tube attached to a slender dowel or long stiff wire will allow a flower with a broken stem to be used in a full arrangement. The dowel will provide the needed height.

Keep a spray bottle of water handy when working with baby's breath. Moistening the florets keeps them from shedding so much.

Hairspray or Design Master's Super Surface Sealer applied to dried baby's breath in arrangements will help keep the florets in place. Do not use hairspray to clean old dried arrangements. It will only glue the dust in place.

A blow drier will quickly dry a tablecloth if water spills from an arrangement.

Save clean jars, whipped topping tubs, plastic microwave dishes, and large plastic tops from detergent bottles to use as liners in containers that cannot hold water.

To clean a glass container and remove old flower residue, fill the container with a glass full of powdered denture cleaner, mixed according to the manufacturer's instructions. I have used several different brands with great success.

Orchid Vial Taped to Dowel or Wire

Wrap the circumference of a ball-shaped candle with a length of embroidered ribbon for added color and texture. In a Christmas design of simple greens, the ribbon will make the candle much more important. Ribbon may be applied over double-faced tape.

DELLA ROBBIA FRUIT WREATH

This handsome fruit centerpiece can be made quickly on a plywood wreath frame that has been painted green. Lay assorted fruit all around the frame, using pieces of double-stick tape or small pieces of floral clay to hold the fruit in place. The fruit must be dry and at room temperature for the mechanics to hold them together. Add a second layer of smaller fruit on the top and sides of the first ring, continuing to use tape or clay to hold them together. Grapes are more easily positioned as a single bunch draped over the top than separated into small clusters. Sprigs of greens, nuts, and berries can fill small holes. Afterward the fruit can be eaten.

A LIVING WREATH

Metal wreath frame
Dark-colored sheet plastic
Potting soil mixed with a little perlite
Sheet moss or sphagnum moss
Light-weight clear fishing line,
   optional
Small plants

This wreath is made from living plants and is suitable for table-top use all year long. The addition of ribbons and special trims will make it festive for Christmas. These wreaths make wonderful gifts as the recipients can enjoy them for a long time.

Purchase a metal wreath frame for the base, and I suggest that it be a small one, 10" to 12", for your first effort because it will require more plant material than you expect. Line the hollow of the frame with one continuous strip of dark-color plastic, which could be cut from a large garbage or trash bag. Keep the plastic down inside the rim of the form by tucking it into place. Fill the form half-way up with a mixture of potting soil and perlite. The addition of perlite to the soil helps to give the plants a little drainage as, technically, there is none.

Remove the little plants from their pots and place them close together around the circumference of the wreath form. Select plants which have similar light, soil, and watering conditions. When the plants are in position, give them a drink of water, but not too much, as heavy watering can cause root rotting very quickly.

Around the outside of the wreath use the sphagnum or sheet moss to cover the plastic, tucking it into place around the plants. If necessary, use fern pins to hold the moss in place. Additional moss may be tucked in between the ribs of the frame on the outside to cover the plastic liner. You may find it helpful to wrap the moss onto the wreath with fine fishing line, and you may choose to perform this step before the plants are inserted into the soil.

Add any trims you may like. Berries are pretty and give color, but you could also use bows, little Santas, small snowmen, or tiny tree balls. Even a few fresh flowers inserted into orchid vials could be pushed into the soil for a temporary garnish. After completing the wreath, I place mine on a clear glass plate to protect the table-top.

As the little plants begin to grow, you will have to keep pinching them back or thinning them out because too much growth will destroy the compact appearance of the wreath. Periodically the plants may have to be replaced. Adding fertilizer to the watering schedule is recommended only in small doses, as you want to keep the plants healthy but you do not want them to grow out of proportion to their surroundings.

A long-lasting living wreath can be created by using varieties of succulents which require strong light but can survive on much less water. The principles of construction are the same, but with succulents use a soil which is more sandy and more to the taste of the cacti and succulents you are using. Ask your local nurseryman to assist you in the proper choice of plants. Succulents need a little more water during their springtime period of growth.

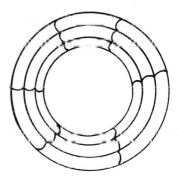

Wire Wreath Frame

Ivy

WINDOW TREATMENTS

The most traditional way to decorate a window for Christmas is to place a lighted electric candle on the inside and hang a wreath on the outside. The overall effect is one of warmth and welcome. The wreath shows to its best advantage during the daylight, and when evening comes the candle takes precedence.

There are other ways, however, to decorate a window. Evergreen roping can be hung outside to frame each window, or draped softly over the top of each window. Trim the inside of a window with a garland of greens decorated with artificial red satin apples and a big bow at the center top.

If there is a wide window sill, Christmas plants could be displayed; but care must be taken that the plants do not get too cold. A lovely arrangement of cut evergreens could be placed on the window sill with no worry about the temperature. If there is no sill, a pedestal displaying a very large arrangement of Christmas flowers and greens is a delight for passers-by. Make it sumptious and overflowing. A combination of dried flowers, freshly-cut greens, and artificial materials might be the solution if you live in a cold area without a storm window.

Christmas tree balls attached to bright ribbons hung at varying lengths is another possible window trim. This is both whimsical and economical. Ribbons and tree ornaments are easy to put up, take down, and store for another year. I suggest unbreakable balls for this purpose.

Large bay windows offer a prominent area to display a Christmas tree, especially pretty at night when the lights are shining. Large pots filled with branches painted white and trimmed with tiny white lights are effective in an oversize window. This gives a glistening snowy appearance appropriate to the season.

If you are a collector of doll houses or miniature objects, make a round shadowbox to fit inside a wreath, and create a mini-Christmas scene in the box. A wonderful object for children to enjoy! This decoration is best for a window facing directly onto a sidewalk because the scene would be too small to be seen from a distance.

What must be avoided in a window design for a sunny location are wax candles, fresh fruit, or candy. Heat from the sun will spoil them, and paper objects fade in the bright sunlight. Avoid the tendency to clutter the window sill with a myriad of unrelated objects. The appearance will be more attractive if there is a purpose in the selection of objects. Keep in mind that the size of any objects on display should be compatible with their location and each other.

FORCING BULBS FOR AFTER-CHRISTMAS COLOR

After all the Christmas decorations have been dismantled and put away, the house takes on an empty air. This is the time for flowering bulbs! You will need to prepare well in advance; however, so all that needs to be done is to bring the forcing pots into the house.

Using instructions given to me by Kitty Washburn, proprietor of Bundles of Bulbs, I have been very successful in forcing flowers into bloom. There are several different ways this can be done.

The first method is done in the refrigerator or another cold, dark, but not freezing, spot such as a window well or an extra garbage can filled with leaves and placed in an unheated attic or basement. The refrigerator must be an extra one because bulbs cannot be forced in a closed area where fruits or vegetables are stored. The temperature should range between 38° and 48° for forcing. Both tulips and daffodils can be forced under these conditions.

Begin the forcing procedure by filling an 8" diameter plastic pot, with several well-spaced open holes in the bottom, with soil or Pro-Mix to about 2/3 full. Place 10 or so tulip or daffodil bulbs into the pot, taking care to have the pointed end of the bulbs up and the rough, rooty end down. Have the flat side of tulip bulbs facing the outer rim of the pot. Cover the bulbs with soil or Pro-Mix.

Place the pot into a sink of water with the level of the water coming at least half-way up the side of the pot. Leave it this way overnight so the soil in the pot becomes well saturated. Next day remove the pot from the water and let it drain. When water stops dripping, the pot can be placed on a saucer and slipped into a clear plastic bag. Do not close the top of the bag. Put the whole thing — pot, saucer, and bag — into a forcing refrigerator, window well, or garbage can with leaves.

Leave the bulbs in the cold darkness for about 13 weeks. This means you must start them the first week of October to have flowers a few weeks after Christmas. Check the moisture of the soil periodically to be certain there is some dampness.

After 13 weeks you may transfer the pot to your living room, giving them only dim light until the shoots are truly green. Then the pot may be moved to a sunny location. Continue to water the bulbs and turn the pot in the light every few days to keep the growth even. After all this, the bulbs will reward you with fragrant beauty during the winter doldrums.

The second method of forcing is done without refrigeration and is very simple — if you use paperwhite narcissus bulbs! Select a deep round bowl or planter without a drainage hole. Fill the bowl with pebbles almost to the top. Place the paperwhite bulbs on top of the pebbles in a pleasing pattern and fill in around them with more pebbles to hold them in place. Do not cover the bulbs with stones. Fill the bowl with water to the level of the base of the bulbs. The roots should be able to touch the water, but the water should not come up as high as the center of the bulb.

Place the bowl of bulbs in a warm and bright, but not sunny location until the leaves are green and growing. Then they may be moved to a sunnier spot. Check the water level every few days to be certain there is enough water for the root systems. Kitty says that 1 tablespoon of gin added to 1 cup of water for one watering will keep the leaves from getting too leggy.

After the flowers appear, I usually move the bulbs out of direct sunshine to make the blooms last a bit longer. When blooming is over, discard the bulbs, wash the pebbles and bowl in hot soapy water, and start another set of bulbs for continuing winter blooms for the house. The blooming time for narcissus 'Galilee' in a guide from the International Dutch Flower Bulb Growers is as follows, when started:

November 15 to 20 - 30 days to bloom
December 15 - about 25 days to bloom
January 15 - about 20 days to bloom

This corner garden of massed house plants was created for a room without a Christmas tree.

DISH GARDEN

A dish garden can be created using almost any shallow-rooted miniature plants. It was finding the delightful ivy-tree topiary that made me
want to make this one. The container is a brass planter lined with plastic
to protect the finish of the metal. The liner was filled with soil and the
planting was completed with a few small variegated ivy plants, moss, holly
sprigs, snowflake chrysanthemums, and woodland figures. After Christmas, the living topiary tree will be returned to its proper container.

INDEX

SOURCES OF SUPPLIES

Apple Cone — The Craft House, Colonial Williamsburg, 201 Fifth Avenue, PO Box CH, Williamsburg, VA 23187

Needlepoint — Fancy Work, 12 Village Square, Village of Cross Keys, Baltimore, MD 21210 (301) 435-9310

Topiary Forms — Topiary, Inc. 41 Bering Street, Tampa, FL 33606 (813) 254-3229

Things you are not able to find elsewhere — Accents, Ltd. Stevenson Village Center, Stevenson, MD 21153 (301) 486-8884